To my beautiful daughter.
And Randy.
Who both put up with a lot for more years than anyone should have to.

AUTHOR DISCLAIMER

The events in this book are remembered to the best of my ability. It should be noted, however, that I was—for the better part of thirteen years—a drug addict. Because of this, I don't always remember all the facts in the exactly right order. Or sometimes, really, any order at all. So, while the stories portrayed in the book are entirely accurate and, while the dialogue is true to the mood and sometimes even to the word, and while I can remember some of the darndest things, like particular outfits I bought at the mall during this period, I cannot always remember big fat chunks of things, like—you know—when things happened. Or how many times I went to jail. Or when any of my court dates or doctor's appointments were supposed to be. Because, although those things are important, they weren't important to me at the time.

Even so, I've done my best to piece together some of the most broken years of my life in a coherent and accurate fashion. That said, there are definitely times when a certain amount of guessing and assuming was involved. Please forgive me for this, as my brain was somewhat fried. Kind of like that commercial. Of your brain. On drugs. Because it was.

Also, I changed everybody's name (almost). And cleaned up the language from my drug days. You're welcome.

All the best—Laura

Therefore if any man be in Christ, he is a new creature; old things are passed away; behold, all things are become new.

— 2 CORINTHIANS

5:17

PROLOGUE

I didn't usually dance, but that night I did. I can't say I danced till I dropped because I never dropped. I had more energy than I'd ever had before. I felt better than I ever had before. Usually when I went out with my friends I was worried about dancing because I didn't want to get hot and sweaty and mess up my hair. I'd tell my girlfriends, "We're just going to stand here and model." Not that night. That night I danced. I danced into the skinny end of the night and into the wide opening of morning. And at the end of it all, I felt great—no regret or concern for what I'd done. At the end of the night, I found myself wondering, "What was I so afraid of?"

Cocaine wasn't a drug that limited you. Cocaine was a drug that set you free. I could dance. I could drink without getting drunk. I could drive safely or go to work. In fact, I could take care of my life just fine—better than fine. Cocaine wasn't a drug that made you pass out. I wasn't spacey or clouded. I didn't see things that weren't there, or lose my inhibitions so that men could take advantage of me. That first night, dancing and then going to parties afterwards, I felt like I could go on forever, live forever, dance forever. And that was a new, and wonderful, feeling for me.

PART I
HAWAII

CHAPTER ONE

I n the '80s, cocaine was everywhere. You could get it at any club or bar, from friends or roommates. And it was relatively cheap. An average line would cost about five dollars (when you broke it down into the price of just one line)—only a bit more than a bottle of wine. Sure a lot of your money would be going to the drug, but not enough that you had to stop.

Celebrities, athletes, and rock stars were all using it, yet it also transcended class—waitresses could buy it just as well as Wall Street businessmen. It was pretty too—white and clean-looking, crystalline and sparkling, powdery as confectioner's sugar—a fairy's drug. It felt fun and friendly. People offered it to you at bars and comedy clubs, at work and play. It was easy to do a line together—like sharing slices of cake. Someone would put a small pile of the pretty white powder on a plate, crumble it as fine as possible, then press it flat with a credit card. After that you would use the card to draw lines through the cocaine; and one by one, everybody would do a line. A circle of friends laughing together.

When I first started doing cocaine, I couldn't see crack

babies screaming in their hospital beds before heading off to over-full foster care, gangs shooting each other, the homicide rate for young black males more than doubling. I couldn't see cocaine-related hospital emergencies on the rise or people dying from overdoses. I couldn't see any statistics at all. When I first started using cocaine, all I could see were happy, working-class people around me. We showed up for our jobs; we paid our taxes; we didn't cheat on our spouses. Life was good.

Especially for someone who was hardly born an angel.

I smoked my first cigarette at age twelve. It was simple— a family friend's house, a cigarette smoldering on an ashtray, a few innocent puffs. In 1972 all beautiful women smoked. That was clear from the ads you saw on TV, from your mother's prettiest friends, from movies and record covers. Any girl who wanted to become a beautiful woman would smoke. And more than almost anything, I wanted to become a beautiful woman. Even if it made me dizzy and sick to my stomach, even if the smoke burned and choked on the way down.

After that first cigarette, I started buying packs for myself.

If you are younger than forty, that might sound crazy, but in the '70s, kids were often sent to buy a pack of cigarettes for their parents. Any child could walk into any gas station or corner store and come out with a pack of cigarettes. Even if there hadn't been an army of gas station attendants willing to hand over the crinkly, square packages to whatever child happened through his doors, there was an army of cigarette vending machines located throughout any major city. Vending machines stood outside of bars and restaurants—the tidy, colorful cigarette boxes lined up in a rainbow assortment like candy. For a mere fifty cents, with the press of a button or the satisfying pull of a lever, any box I chose would fall from its bondage and into my twelve-year-old hands.

By the time I was fourteen, I was hooked. I needed a cigarette in the morning, on the way to school, at lunch, and on the way home. I would find times to sneak out and have one. When I took a shower, I found I could grab a quick smoke. The window in the bathroom was behind the toilet, so I'd stand there—behind the toilet—with the window open, blowing smoke out into the open air—just a few puffs and I'd put it out, just enough to get me through until I could smoke a full cigarette later.

When my parents found out, my father made me stand in front of him and smoke a whole pack as punishment, thinking it would make me sick enough that I would never do it again. But by that time the only thing that bothered me about smoking a pack of cigarettes was that he had bought Winstons when I preferred menthols. As I smoked, my brother, Randy, held a handkerchief in front of my mouth and told me to blow into it. The handkerchief came away yellow and tarred. "That's the crap that's going into your lungs," he said. Yup. And I wasn't stopping.

I started drinking at age fifteen. My dad was stationed at the Hickam Air Force Base, right by Pearl Harbor. This meant that I spent my teenage years surrounded by attractive men in uniform who were just a few years older than I was. My friend used to drive her father's electric blue mustang convertible all around the island. She was a fiery redhead, green-eyed, and tan. I was a smooth-skinned brunette with doe-like brown eyes, fair skin, and perfect teeth. We were young, we were beautiful, and we looked dangerously older than we were. We wanted to act older too. When we wanted to drink, we'd drive to any liquor store and I would get out, comb through my purse in front of the building and then, as soon as a man came near me, I would start in, "Oh crap. I forgot my license. Do you think you could just pick something up for us?" They always did. Every single time. Back then I wasn't as dependent on the wine as I was on the thrill of the lie, the manipulation, the power of getting someone to do something for me that they probably knew they shouldn't do. Back then the wine wasn't for a buzz. It was an act of independence, of willfulness, of power and beauty. To act older, to grow up faster, to rebel.

MY SOPHOMORE YEAR IN HIGH SCHOOL I MET SANKA. HE WAS a Hawaiian surfer with long shoulder-length black hair, a puka shell necklace, and bronze perfect skin. He was a life-guard at my favorite beach. Or, I suppose, it was my favorite beach because Sanka was there. We'd had minor flirtations, exchanged phone numbers, called one another. Even so we'd never gone out, not even to catch a movie together. But that Christmas break when my father grounded me, probably for my grades, I ran away in the middle of the night, took the bus across the island, found Sanka, and stayed with him in his house. If this was a piece of juicy, sordid fiction, I'd tell you all kinds of juicy, sordid details about my few days in Sanka's apartment. The truth, however, is almost disappointingly boring. I slept in his bed without ever once sleeping with him. I ate his food. And when he found out how old I was, he told me that I needed to go home.

I'd been gone for several days. My parents had called everyone they could think of and were looking for me all over the island. When you've terrified your parents to this level, it's kind of terrifying to go back. I didn't feel like I could call my mother and tell her where I was or that I wanted to come home. Instead, I did the only thing I saw as a perfectly safe option. I called my mother's preacher, Pastor Smith. He wouldn't kill me or start sobbing into the phone; he wouldn't tell me what a horrible mess I was and how I was wrecking his life. He would be kind, but firm, welcoming, but warning. And he was. He called my parents, came and got me, and I went home.

In some ways after that, it was a changed home. My parents watched me more closely, threatened me more seriously. After that, I realize when I look back, I was flagged—the child who would make the most bad decisions, the child who would break her parents' hearts.

It took me a few years, but I didn't let them down.

CHAPTER TWO

Me and my dad

I moved out of my parents' house three days before my eighteenth birthday. We were living in Florida by then and back in 1978, you could buy booze at age eighteen, which meant you could tend bars at that age too. That was the quickest path I saw to fast, easy money, to a young adulthood of simple independence. And I took it. It got even easier ten months later when, driving home from work, I wrecked my car. When the check from my insurance company came, I used the money to buy a one-way ticket to go back to Hawaii.

My dad upgraded it to a two-way ticket. "You'll be back," he said with all the cocky confidence of an adored parent.

He was wrong.

DESPITE MY BEST EFFORTS TO WIND UP IN JUVENILE HALL, MY father and I had always been close. When I was young, he would buy me a new outfit, then take me out on a "date" to dinner at his work—a night club where he worked part-time as the bouncer. He'd order dinner and buy me a Shirley Temple, which I would sip from that tall, cold, grown-up glass. I loved my dad. And he loved me. Truthfully, we shared a lot of the same vices. We liked beautiful, sophisticated, worldly things. We drank. We smoked on the sly. We didn't like to be tied down. Thus, despite the fact that I worried him to death—maybe even because I worried him to death—he tended to favor and protect me. I was his only girl. I adored him. An easy child for my father to love, if not an easy child for my father to bring up. Throughout my life, he had asked only one thing of me—one unequivocal request: he didn't want me to ever try drugs. He'd seen lives ruined and he said drugs would ruin mine. When your dad only asks one thing of you, you should be able to do it. Right?

And so, despite all the other bad girl stuff I liked to do, I never accepted a joint from a friend, never took the lines that were offered to me several times a night at the bar where I worked in Hawaii. Never raided a pill cabinet or snuck some of my roommate's stash. I drank every night after work, then went to the clubs that were still open and drank some more. I tried as many cocktail combinations as my co-workers could dream up. I smoked till my throat burned dry. I woke up every morning to a Diet Pepsi and a cigarette, and fell asleep to the tune of tequila's bitter last call. Still, I could resist the powders and pouches and hastily rolled doobies with a strange kind of Puritan determination. At least I did until I was twenty-one years old.

Maybe that doesn't sound very long, but when you're offered two lines every night at work for three and a half years, when your roommate is heavily addicted to cocaine and wants you to be too, when all of these drugs are offered to you for free, often by attractive men, then three years starts to stretch on. Three years means that I turned down at least 2,184 lines before I finally accepted one.

Such a small infraction.

A nibble, a glance, a breath, moment, instant.

2,184 versus 1.

It sounds impressive when you put it that way, doesn't it? It wasn't. It wasn't impressive. The end result was the same. It was the top of a slippery slope. I got out my sled.

Peg had been my roommate for eight months. We worked together and drank together. She'd been using cocaine for years and she really wanted me to join in the fun. I really didn't. I wasn't always smart, but I was smart enough to know I didn't need another bad habit. I resisted through eight months of pressuring and cajoling.

And then one night we went to a concert. It was the Jackson Five Reunion concert in Waikiki and we were late—not fashionably late, but very late. The cover band was done and the Jackson Five had already started. I hated to be late. I hated walking into a packed place, hated not being able to find seats or space, unable to enjoy the thing I'd paid for.

I was trying to hustle Peg out of my car. It was a brand-new Cadillac El Dorado—two-tone, black and silver with a sun roof, and soft gray velour interior. I'd special-ordered my car and waited four months to get it. I loved that car. There was no way I would leave it without locking it up. But Peg wouldn't get out. She wanted me to do a line with her—just a tiny little line. She sat there stubbornly in my passenger seat, refusing to leave till I tried it.

"I'm not going to try it," I said.

"You'll like it," she argued, all sweet good nature.

"I know I'll like it," I said. "That's why I'm not going to try it."

"Oh, just try it," she said, like she did almost every day, but this time she added, "Try it just this once and I'll never ask you to do it again."

Now that *was* a deal. Peg pestered me to do a line with her several times a week. It was irritating and tiring to keep turning her down. Plus, there was no way I was going to leave Peg in my new car so she could get out in an hour, walk away, and leave it unlocked.

"You promise?" I asked.

"Promise," she said. I slipped back into the driver's seat while Peg corn-rowed two neat lines of the silky white powder on the back of a plastic cassette tape cover.

Looking back, it seems strange—and would be funny (if it wasn't)—how I was willing to trade my life to get to the Jackson Five Reunion concert. If I were to have asked someone in 1981 what they would give to go to a Jackson Five Reunion concert, they probably wouldn't have said fifteen hundred dollars every month, an abusive boyfriend, a molested child, a lost family, hotels for houses, a ruined leg, a gun to my head, a knife to my butt, a jail cell all my own, black eyes, bruised days, broken hours. Most people probably wouldn't have given that to be on time to a Jackson Five Reunion concert.

But I did.

It only took four seconds.

THEY CALL IT THE MORNING AFTER. THAT'S NOT A VERY accurate term. It's usually well into the afternoon when you finally wake up. The morning is spent racing the dawn home so you can tumble into your apartment at 4:00 am—pupils dilated, high and buzzy. Of course, then you need a couple more hours to drink yourself down from the high. At about seven you fall into a dead, dreary sleep—tossing and dreaming before waking after all the morning bells have tolled so you can get ready to go to your job.

I guess I was lucky that I didn't have to be at work until 2:00 in the afternoon because that next day I felt more tired than I'd ever felt in my life. Tired is not even the right word for it. Everyone knows tired. This was different. It was like recovering from the flu and running a marathon and having a baby. It was like nothing I'd ever felt before. It was deeper than a hangover, darker than a sleepless night. It was exhaustion at a level I'd never known.

Lucky for me, there was a simple fix.

Because the one thing I didn't have after my first time using cocaine was a strong sense of regret. It bugged me that I'd broken the rule for myself. But after that rule had been broken, it seemed a little like losing your virginity. You can't go back. So I figured, "Why try?" I didn't have a sense of repair or the feeling that now I should make a fresh start and not do it again. The only thing I really felt was that it hadn't been so bad. Who was I kidding? It had been incredible. There was never a real question about whether or not I would take cocaine again. Of course I would. It had given me more energy, vitality, and clarity than I'd ever felt before. And right then—exhausted and needing to get to work—some energy and clarity would be useful. I was used to taking medicine, caffeine, and alcohol to fill my needs and holes. My dad, with all his anti-drug talk, had been the one to teach me that there was a pill for every ill. That morning I was tired. That morning I was beyond anything that tired ever was. This "pill" would fix that just fine.

Peg lent me a little coke to get me through the day. And then we started buying it together—so friendly, so economical to share. Peg was thrilled. I was like, "Whatever." The truth was that I didn't really think it would matter that much in the large and long scheme of things. Life would roll on.

And it did. For me anyway. Several years later, Peg died in a car accident. I don't know if she was high or low, but she was always something. She wouldn't have to live through the consequences of a life on drugs. I would. But for now, I was just getting started.

I DON'T KNOW HOW LONG IT TOOK BEFORE I COULDN'T NOT take it. It was around every day, and often it didn't cost me anything because men gave it to me. So I just took it—a little kid with a free sucker from the bank. Four months in, the highs started to level off, started to feel a lot more like normals, which meant I needed more drug. Six months in, I started slipping on my bills—nothing major—just a late payment here, forgot the water bill there. I never got kicked out of my apartment or lost power. It's just that I found myself distracted, preoccupied. After a year, I would think, "I'm just not going to buy it tomorrow." But I would. Every time. The thing was that all the people around me were doing it too, feeling the same way, struggling with the same thing. It made it seem normal, connective even. We all had our problems. Sure. That was just life.

Eight months after I started, I was buying a half gram a day. When people ask me how many lines that was, I can't tell them. It was a lot—six or seven-ish. I did one in the morning, several throughout the course of the day. And always at work. We didn't necessarily do lines either. To do a line, you had to go into the bathroom and snort it off the back of the toilet seat. Which wasn't my favorite method. Sometimes when we wanted to do it in the open, we'd keep it in a bag, then pass it around. You'd insert a skinny little cocktail straw that had been cut in half. Fill the straw with an inch of cocaine, stick it up your nose, and snort. Quick, inconspicuous, effective. No toilet needed. Then you'd pass the bag to someone else, or tuck it away for later. In this way I lost track of lines done, grams done, drugs done. I just stayed awake. I drank as much as I wanted. It was the way you partied. It was the way you lived. Life.

***

COCAINE WAS DEFINITELY MY DRUG OF CHOICE. BUT WHEN you're drinking and wasted and used to using cocaine to pick you up, you can get into trouble, accidentally trying other drugs. In that first year of drug use, where I learned I could drink myself to the point of being wasted, then do a line or two to take off the drunk, I was at a party, trashed and drinking with friends. I was utterly, completely drunk. They were passing around a mirrored plate. To me, a mirrored plate meant just one thing. I did half a line and asked a friend what it was. I was still very drunk—so drunk that I couldn't really feel the full effects of this new drug. Still, I could tell that it made me feel amazing.

"China White," my friend said.

I didn't know what that was, but I said, "I want more of that stuff."

A few days later my friend got me a little bit more. It was less than fifty dollars. I was at the Atlantis nightclub in Hawaii. I took it into the bathroom, sat backwards on the toilet seat and chopped it up on the back of the toilet. It looked just like cocaine with its pearly white lines. But it wasn't cocaine. As soon as I did a line, my head fell backwards, my neck like rubber, my muscles completely relaxed. Like I was floating in the clouds. Everything was beautiful. Just being there in the bathroom was the purest pleasure I had ever experienced. I couldn't walk. I must have stayed on that public toilet for a very long time. Which was fine with me. I never wanted to leave, never wanted that feeling to change or go away. I'm not sure how long I was there; I'm not sure how I left the bathroom or the bar or got home.

The third time I asked for China White, my friend was evasive. "You can't mess too much with that stuff," he said. "You're gonna turn into a heroin addict."

"I've never done heroin," I said.

"China White is heroin," he replied.

I wasn't sure I believed him. I didn't want to believe him. Heroin was scary. Heroin was corpse-like people slumped on the street with a needle in their arm. "You have to shoot heroin," I said.

"No. It's definitely heroin," he said. "That stuff can ruin your life so fast. I've seen people torn apart from heroin use."

Still, I'm not sure that that knowledge would have been enough to stop me, except that he said, "They don't have any more. It's gone." Maybe it was. Maybe he was just protecting his own butt. Or maybe he was trying to help me. Either way, he saved me. He was my only source; there was no other way for me to get it. All drugs will eat you up—bite by bite—violent, but subtle. But heroin will consume you like fire—flesh to ash.[1]

Through the years, I would see people snort it, chew it, even smoke it. Chasing the Dragon. That's what they called it. That's what it was—the pursuit of something they would never find. They folded aluminum foil in half—shiny side down.[2]

In the center of the folded foil, they'd put the crystalline drug. Then they'd fold it again like a simple bird—creased center, "wings" bent outward. The drug was at one end of the crease. They'd put a Bic lighter under that and melt the drug, which would drip down the fold. At the end, they'd inhale the smoke that wafted up the crease with a straw.

I understood it—why people chased the dragon. I understood how people got hooked after just one use. My trip on heroin was just what people say it is—puppy dogs and rainbows. But more. Better. Everything good you've ever known, every feeling you've ever wanted to have. I can see how people say it is the closest they've felt to heaven. Maybe that's partly what justifies more use. How could something that takes you to a place so sublime be bad? And yet, of all the drugs I've seen used, heroin is the worst one. Because you can never achieve the same euphoria again. It is a drug that gives once—so fully and perfectly that most people will do anything to experience it again, but they never can. Which is why it takes you so quickly from heaven to hell. They call it "dope sick" when you're coming off of heroine. It's a physical sickness; it's a mental sickness. Many people feel they can never come off of it, and so they use it again and again, always wishing for that first euphoria, never getting it, soon barely maintaining any level of normal mood or happiness despite heavy use.

Seeing junkies stumble around with their arms a mess of scar tissue, it was easy to see—that no matter what it felt like —heroine wasn't something that came from the angels. Still, seeing and believing are different things, and I'm not sure I would have stopped if my friend hadn't cut me off. But he did. After that, I went back to regular partying with regular cocaine.

---

1. Sometimes within weeks, new addicts will suffer from extreme weight loss, gaunt faces, scabs, pitted complexions, and tooth loss. And that's just how they look on the outside.
2. They did this because the other side would create a toxic reaction. Kind of ironic, really, for people to worry about toxins when doing heroin, but they did.

CHAPTER THREE

I n 1981, a year after Brooke Shield's steamy *Endless Love* came out, a white girl in Hawaii with brown hair, brown eyes, strong features and good skin was more than a novelty. She was a prize. Men loved me.

Me at age 22

When they came in, they would ask me to wait their tables. "Hey Brooke," they'd call. Or, "We want Brooke."[1] They'd leave large tips, ask me out to dinner, buy me drinks.

My favorite restaurants were Nick's Fish Market and John Dominus, both of which would rack up an easy two hundred dollar tab. For this my date would get a peck on the cheek and, if he was lucky, a promise for another date. If I told them I couldn't go out because I didn't have anything to wear, they'd take me on a shopping trip for a new outfit. Often, without so much as a first date, these men would bring me presents—jewelry and flowers. At first, I hesitated to take things, and then one of my girlfriends said, "Hey. If they don't give it to you, they'll just give it to someone else." In that way, I guess it kind of went along with our creeds for life. Take what you can get when it's offered. It might not be there tomorrow.

Sometimes people on the mainland don't believe me when I tell them this; they figure there must have been more to it. After all, what guy is going to hang around, take you to nice restaurants and buy you jewelry for no more than a peck on the cheek? But for a petite, pretty Brooke Shields looka-like in Hawaii, it was something you could expect. Men would pay—just for a chance. And they did.

Maybe I should have taken some of those chances— found a nice guy, settled down. But I didn't want to. My Cadillac had a bumper sticker that read, "Single and loving it." Ironically, it was a man magnet. Men would drive along-side me, cat call me, try to talk to me. If they'd really wanted a girl, they should have chased after someone with a bumper sticker that said, "Single and wants to get married soon." But nobody ever did. They wanted me. I didn't want them back, but I wouldn't complain about the attention. I'd never been that popular before.

TWO YEARS AFTER I STARTED DOING DRUGS, TIM WALKED into my life. He was more than ten years older than me, Polynesian, a little pot-bellied, not my type at all. He came into the bar where I worked with a bunch of his friends. They asked me to wait their table and after a few drinks, they told me that they'd been missing Tim—he'd just gotten out of prison. His friends were indignant—he never should have been sent there, they told me. And it seemed to be true. Tim might not have been hot, but he was charming, funny, and so nice. How could a guy like that be sent to a state penitentiary on the mainland? It seemed impossible. He'd been there, I was told, for tax evasion. Tax evasion. It was just too ridiculous to lock a nice guy like that up for missing a few tax payments.

Later, much later, I would learn that often law enforcement got drug pushers and mafia leaders locked up on small charges—things they could pin them down for, things they could prove, things like evading taxes. But I didn't know that when Tim walked into my life. I just knew that a nice, funny guy had plunked down at one of my tables. I also knew, couldn't help but notice, that he didn't seem to pay me nearly as much attention as the other men at the bar. There was something about that that got to me—I wanted him to notice me, to ask me out to dinner, to swoon in the ways it seemed everyone else did.

He might not have swooned, but Tim, his friends and I still fell into an easy pattern of going out together after I got done with work. We'd head away from the tourist district to the slower, more low-key nightclubs with local bands and native Hawaiians—listening to music, drinking, and getting high. It was true that Tim and I were spending a lot of time together, but he never made a pass at me or even tried to kiss me. One night, at my door, I paused, waiting. Nothing. He just walked out. That night, I realized how much I had wanted something. I told my friend, "You know, I think I kind of like him."

"A lot of girls do," she said.

"He's not even my type," I said.

"I know," she said. "He just has a way about him."

And he did. Whenever we walked into bars together, people stopped, said hello. It was like the sea parted—smiling faces on either side. I loved being with a man who commanded so much respect. And I loved being with a man who made me laugh.

One night, in a move that would fill me up and then empty me out a thousand times over, my friend told Tim that I liked him. Apparently, he liked me too. That night when I got off work, he leaned close. I leaned closer. After that everything changed. After that, we couldn't be separated. I stopped going out with my girlfriends. Tim took all my time, all my thoughts, all my energy. I'd never fallen in love before and, like I did with everything else, I didn't bother going halfway.

Three months into our relationship, we were spending every night together—going out, getting high, then heading back to one of our apartments. One night we were going to Tim's apartment. He drove up to it slowly, as though looking for something. And then, casually, he said, "You know, I don't want to go there tonight. Let's stay at a hotel."

It seemed sexy, romantic, to get ourselves our own cozy room. Weirdly, though I didn't bother to think about it at the time, Tim had already checked in. Or at least he already had the key. He had a reason for it of course. Tim always had a reason. His cousin was in town and staying there too. His friend had planned to stay there, and had already paid for the room, but he couldn't stay there tonight, so it was open. Lucky us.

We settled in, already high as birds and buzzed as bees. It was easy to forget back then how much we did drugs. But the truth was that we were always a little high, sometimes a lot high. If we weren't high, we were low and we were wanting, aching, waiting to get high. It got to the point where it didn't seem so strange, or bad at all—just seemed like part of the day—the way other people think about sleep or food. Sure you get hungry. It's what a human body does. And when you're hungry, you eat. No one would fault you for that. No one would call it weakness or addiction. That was how my life felt with drugs. Sure, I used them. Sure, I kind of needed them. But they were just part of my day—as normal as a cup of coffee in the morning.

What wasn't normal was the small safe at the far end of the hotel room. Tim opened it and there, inside, were four large bricks of drugs. I remember watching him take them out of the safe—like slabs of perfectly white cheese. He cut a sliver off of one. That would be for us. The rest he put into a small briefcase, which he returned to the safe. It was crazy. Dangerous. Scary. But also kind of exciting—powerful—to have so much drug, so much money, sitting in a nice hotel room like nothing at all. Looking at those bricks was like looking at thousands of dollars that had been purified, concentrated, and then compacted together.

I didn't want to get caught with that much cocaine on our hands, but I was still more than happy to take the line that Tim gave me. At the time, the pretty powder was just a toy to me—something to play with after work, something to give me energy when I didn't have any. Even with that briefcase of cocaine sitting in the same room with me, I didn't know how a drug could take over a life. At that point, my drug habit was just that—a habit, maybe even a bad habit, but a habit over which I still maintained some small degree of control. Each year, visiting my parents in Florida for two weeks, I would stop. Girls I knew weren't selling sex to get it. Men I knew weren't dropping dead from overdoses. People I knew still cared about other people, as did I. I didn't see how any drug could change that. I didn't realize then how an addiction could branch out so that soon enough it wasn't just the drug controlling you but the lies, the crime, the lost opportunities, the criminal records, the failing health—silken braids of need that would wrap around you until they either choked you or you fought free.

Tim and I didn't sleep, just sat on the bed with our drugs and our drinks—incredibly high, taking risks, being in love. And then something in Tim flipped. Over the years, I've tried to remember what caused it, what created that change this first time, what brought out the animal in the person I loved, the person I knew loved me. But I can't remember—wasn't sober enough to remember. Later it would be jealousy about another guy, or irritation at something I didn't do right. But that first night—I still can't tell you what made him snap. All I know is that it took only seconds. And then Tim was punching me, close fisted, in the face.

I'd never so much as been slapped by my mother, much less struck in the face by a man. He threw me on the bed, holding my hair with one hand while he hit me repeatedly with the other. He hit my eyes, my nose, my lips and cheeks. Once a friend asked me to describe how he hit me. I told her that he didn't hit me; he beat me. He punched me, tore out my hair, pinned me down on the bed until flashes stabbed into my vision, bursts of stars falling from the sky. I thought he would kill me. I was trapped in a strange hotel room. I was small. I was high. I didn't dare scream—there were thousands of dollars' worth of drugs in the room and if we got caught we would go to jail.

Just as I don't remember how it started, I don't remember how it ended. But it did. Tim left the hotel room—maybe to get a smoke, maybe to walk it off.

My face was red and bruising—my eyes turning to circles of oil, one completely swollen shut, the other red and shot through with blood. Chunks of my hair had been ripped out. I stumbled from the hotel room, ran into Tim's cousin who was visiting from L.A., and told him what had happened. He couldn't believe it. Neither could I. I couldn't believe that Tim had hurt me when I knew he loved me. But he had. And I was done with it. I took a cab home, determined never to see or speak with him again.

In three days I was supposed to fly to Florida for my grandmother's funeral. I called my mother, fed her a lie. I don't remember the exact lie, though it must have been a very good lie—maybe I'd gotten in a car accident, maybe I'd been mugged and my driver's license stolen. Whatever it was had been so terrible that I couldn't make the flight, not when I was supposed to; whatever it was was terrible enough that my mother accepted the excuse without question. But none of it was as terrible as what had really happened.

I spent the day of my grandmother's funeral pent up in my apartment, letting the oil spots of my eyes drift from black to purple, and then in the next week from blue to green. I called in sick to work. I avoided going anywhere. I was embarrassed that something like this had happened. *Embarrassed*. It seems like the wrong word to use. Embarrassed is what happens when you stumble on the sidewalk, when you forget an acquaintance's name, when you mix up an order at work. Embarrassed is not when you're beaten black and blue. And yet, when I thought about leaving my apartment, going to work, facing my family, I could find no better word to describe the way I felt. Embarrassed: 1) to cause confusion and shame, 2) to make difficult or intricate, 3) to put obstacles or difficulties in the way of; impede.[2] Embarrassed was me.

---

1. I did *not* look just like Brooke Shields. But in the predominantly Asian/Polynesian culture of Hawaii, I was good enough.
2. http://www.dictionary.com/browse/embarrassed

CHAPTER FOUR

Addictions, you may notice, came easy to me. And, interestingly, when you're addicted to drugs, it becomes easy to be addicted to other things—money, food, relationships.

Tim's cousin started calling me first. He was a nice guy and I liked him. He was furious with Tim for what he'd done to me. Interestingly, that made him the perfect person to advocate for Tim. Tim, he told me apologizing, was an idiot. Tim, he told me, didn't know how it had happened himself. Tim, he told me, was a wreck over what he'd done and would never do it again. I should talk to Tim—Tim Tim Tim. Tim was a mess; Tim felt horrible. What I should have said, what I wish a million times that I'd said was, "Tim's a wreck? Where are his bloody eyeballs; where are his missing clumps of hair?" "Tim feels horrible? Where is his bruised neck, his aching scalp, his eye sealed closed?" But I didn't say any of that. What I did eventually say was, "Fine. Pass the phone. I'll talk to him."

The first time I talked to Tim, he was in tears, torn up like I'd never heard him, sniveling like a child, like a baby who could never, would never hurt a person again. He apologized over and over. He told me he didn't know how it had happened, that it would never happen again. He swore to me that he would rather cut off his arm than ever hit me again.

Even now, after all these years, I believe that in that moment he was sincere. I believe that, even amidst the lies that had built up the scaffolding of his life, he truly meant what he said that day—that he would rather cut off his arm than strike me again. Of course sincerity and action are two different things, sometimes so difficult to line up that even the best of people spend most of their lives perfecting the practice. But at age twenty-three, I didn't realize that. All I knew was that he loved me. And I loved him. What could I do? By the time my face had healed, I was ready to see him again. I'd intended to re-enter the relationship slowly, carefully, eyes wide open. But as soon as he showed up at my house, I opened the door, then shut it behind us. We were together again.

TWO WEEKS LATER I BOARDED A FLIGHT, VISITED MY parents. My mother took me in for an OB appointment as she always did when I visited, insistent on trying to keep me healthy despite my best efforts to thwart her. I was still on the crinkly paper of the examination table when the pregnancy test came back positive. A delicate life was growing in my womb. A tiny, tiny baby. I was thrilled. So was Tim. We would make things right. We would create good things together. Life would go on. Life would be good.

BUT YOU'VE HEARD THIS STORY BEFORE, HAVEN'T YOU? AND you already know how it ends.

LIFE WITH TIM WASN'T GOOD. NOT EVEN A LITTLE. I QUIT drinking and doing drugs for the duration of my pregnancy, though I ached for the day the baby would be born and I could do them again. I stopped working as soon as I started to show. The feminists in the house might not understand this, but—simply put—you never saw a pregnant cocktail wait-ress. I wasn't about to be the first.

The months after that were long and lonely. My belly got bigger and, since my social life had consisted of doing lines and chugging drinks, my circle of friends dropped to zero. I had nothing to do. We got a new townhouse—big enough that we could fit comfortably when the baby came, though we would never fit, never be comfortable.

Tim was often out—partying with his friends or "getting money" though he had no job. I didn't question it though. We needed money and for the first time since I was twelve, I wasn't making any. Consequently, every time he came back with money from whatever not-job he had, I wasn't suspi-cious or angry as I should have been; I was relieved.

Or as close to relieved as you can be when you're trapped in the four walls of your own life. Interestingly, I didn't feel trapped by my baby at all. I felt trapped by the apartment, the emptiness of my bank account, my lack of friends, my depen-dence on someone who was—it was increasingly obvious —*not* going to cut off his hand before hitting me again.

THE SECOND TIME TIM BEAT ME WAS IN A NIGHT CLUB. NOT just any club, but an after-hours bar, which—in case you're wondering—isn't a legal thing. Some bars would stay open serving drinks even when they should have stopped. People would stay there drinking, doing drugs, and gambling—the perfect environment for a young mother-to-be. I sat there sipping a club soda, envying everyone else's drinks when Tim went off on me again. This time, he dragged me into the office and beat me there. After that there were always reasons. He saw me looking at another guy. I made his sandwich with tomatoes which I knew he hated. I folded the towels the wrong way. Every beating as bad as the first. But his apologies came less often and with less conviction. Often when he came at me, he would say, "You know what you did." But I didn't. I never had any idea what he was talking about.

When I was eight months pregnant, we invited his best friend over for dinner. This was a man so close to Tim that our daughter would have his name as her middle name. Dinner was fine. I managed not to put tomatoes near Tim; and the napkins, apparently, were adequately folded. After his friend left, however, Tim cornered me in the kitchen. "I saw the way you looked at him," he said, backing me against the wall. I was eight months pregnant. I wasn't looking at anything but the exit.

I tried to keep Tim calm, to coax him down from his fury. Sometimes this was something I could do, take him back from the edge, from the madness that piled up inside of him. I couldn't that day. He took me into the bedroom, threw me onto the bed, started choking me, then pounded into my face like it was a deadly spider he was determined to kill.[1] Our windows were open and I tried to scream as he did this, but my voice was raspy from being choked. Any time I got a gasp out, I said, "Help me. Somebody. Help." People walked by, but they couldn't hear me. No one stopped or called the cops.

I wound up at the ER that night—almost dead, but not quite broken. They told me to go to a shelter. I would not. I would not leave my car and clothes and furniture in his possession.[2] When I left, it would be with the parts of me that I had brought.

PHOEBE CAME INTO MY LIFE SEVEN WEEKS LATER AND THREE weeks overdue. The night I went into labor, Tim was downstairs with a friend getting high while I lay in our room watching a movie called "The Burning Bed"—a true life story about a woman so abused by her husband that eventually she poured gasoline around his bed and set the house on fire. It was not a funny story. But I was laughing—laughing so hard my water broke.

Thirty-eight hours and a C-section later Phoebe left the safety of my womb and came into the chaos of my life. I was determined to protect her from it. She was the most beautiful thing I had ever seen—an orb of bright light in the windowless room my life had become. I was already plotting to leave; Phoebe would come with me. It was something, at last, to look forward to.

The other thing I looked forward to was the chance to get high again. It was such a relief, like an old comfortable friend had come back to town. You might think a little better of me if I told you that it was the stress of my life, my helplessness, my frustration that pushed me back to my old habits. Unfortunately, I can't tell you that. The truth was that I'd always known pregnancy was just a pause, a break before I went back to doing something that I loved, that I had missed.

I didn't consider my drug use a part of my main problem. I didn't even consider it a corollary to it. For whatever reasons, I couldn't yet connect the dots—drugs lead to wrong man lead to that man doing illegal things regarding drugs lead to dependence on drugs for money lead to that man being psychologically stressed lead to that man beating me lead to me not even remembering why it had started lead to unexpected pregnancy and on and on. It would be years before I would connect any of those dots, years before I would stop accusing bad luck of randomly and cruelly tapping me on the shoulder and asking me to dance.

By the time Phoebe was born, I'd been waiting months to do a line and have a drink. I didn't want to wait any longer. But I was careful. I bottle fed Phoebe, so she would not be exposed to any drug. I did the drugs at home, not at clubs in the middle of the night. After my hiatus, I didn't need as much drug and used it less frequently. I put my daughter first as well as I knew how.

Which meant getting my butt out of the widening hell that was my life.

The problem was that it would take time. In the span of a few short months as my passionate love for Tim had flipped its head into a hatred just as deep, I'd gone from a financially independent single woman to an abused mother with no money, job, or skills. I didn't feel like I could tell my parents or friends anything—couldn't let them see that out of the wide gamut of men who'd been interested in me, I had managed to pick the very worst one—the one who would not bring me gifts and take me to dinner, who would not buy me outfits and fawn over my hair. No, I'd picked the one who would beat me until I felt my skull would break in half—that one.[3] But I had a plan.

Each day I took Phoebe to the mall. Often I'd meet a friend there—by accident or on purpose. Either way, I'd always mention how tight money was, how I needed a little cash for diapers or formula or food, just to get us through. Hawaiians are generous people. The friends I met were always willing to slip me a ten, a twenty or more.[4] In my car,

I had a box of envelopes stamped and addressed to my dad. As soon as I got the cash, I would fold it into a blank piece of paper and mail it to him. I'd told him I was trying to save money and asked him to deposit the money into an account for me so I wouldn't accidentally spend it. He knew I was a lousy saver, so he didn't question why I might be sending random bills from Hawaii to Florida for him to put in the bank. It only took six months for me to have thousands of dollars saved.

Me with baby Phoebe

Phoebe

Mom with Phoebe

Which was good. Life—as it likes to do—was getting complicated. When I was pregnant, my right knee had started bothering me. I didn't think too much about it—I'd gained about forty pounds during my pregnancy. But after a few more months, a simple tap on that knee was enough to send excruciating pain shooting through my leg.

After Phoebe was born, I went to the doctor. He diagnosed it as synovial chondromatosis—tiny hard formations that spread through my knee like bits of coral. Sometimes these bits broke free and then rolled around like marbles in my joint. Three months after Phoebe was born, I had my first of many surgeries. They cut several small holes in my knee and removed the coral-like pieces, then stitched me up and sent me home with a pair of crutches and a prescription for Tylox.

This worked for a few months. I returned to work part time, but soon enough the "corals" were growing again and, with them, the pain in my leg. The surgery had to be repeated.

I took my Tylox religiously. It's important to point out that I never considered myself addicted to the medicine, nor did I use it outside the instructions marked on the bottle. In fact, I was very careful to keep it within the limits. I could take one pill every four to six hours. I took that pill on the clock every four hours. If the weekend was coming I'd dump out my pill bottle and make sure I had enough to get me through the weekend. And by "get me through" I mean if I didn't have enough to take my pill every four hours through the weekend until Monday at eight in the morning when the pharmacy opened, if I would even find myself one pill short of this, I would call the doctor on Friday and tell him I needed my prescription refilled because I didn't have enough to make it through.

I never considered skipping a pill or breaking one in half or stretching it out by taking the pills at five or six hour intervals. No. I would call and have the prescription refilled. I couldn't risk not having it, not even for a few hours. I needed it. It was too much to deal with the physical pain in my knee when everything else in my life (except for my daughter) was also so painful.

Since the corals kept re-growing, the doctors kept repeating the surgeries. After the Tylox, they bumped me up to Valium—the yellow, and then the stronger blue pills. And then Percocet. All in all, I went through twelve knee surgeries, which lasted over the course of seven years. After several surgeries, my doctor looked through his paperwork and made a simple observation: "You've been on these pain pills for a long time."

Um, yeah, because I'd been in pain for a long time.

He continued, "I can't keep giving you this. You've been on it way too long. You're certainly addicted by now."

That was ridiculous. I was addicted to plenty of things. I knew how addiction worked. With addiction you *wanted* something that wasn't good for you. This was different. Medicine wasn't something you wanted; it was something you *needed*.

The doctor wrote me a prescription for methadone. I knew what that was, and I didn't want to take it. Methadone was what doctors gave heroin addicts when they were trying to wean them from the drug. I told my doctor, "I can't get that. When I go to the pharmacy I'll look like a heroin addict." It would be humiliating.

"We'll get you off this gradually. You'll take less and less over time. It won't last forever."

I still didn't want to show up at the pharmacy looking like a junkie, but I got my prescription anyway.

Then one night I popped my pills out at work. "You can get methadone," one of the girls said. "Give me some. You can get twenty dollars a pill for those." The girls were almost fighting over them. I didn't give anyone any that night. Or ever.

I went home and flushed them down the toilet. The embarrassment of picking up my prescription was bad enough. Having people fight over them and pressure me to get more and then whine and cry if I gave one to someone and not someone else—it was just too much. I got rid of them. Now no one could get mad at me if I didn't give it to them. It was over. Done.

That weekend I had the worst flu of my life. I fell asleep and within an hour had soaked through my sheets and the mattress pad with sweat. I stripped the bed, too tired to do anything, but throw a blanket under me, though in almost no time I had soaked through that too. When the vomiting started, it got so severe that I had to crawl hand and knee to the bathroom where I would puke and have diarrhea at the same time, then lie there shivering before crawling back to my bed, soaking through another blanket, and then doing it all again.

Years later, when I saw a friend coming off heroin—shaking, vomiting, dizzy, I would realize that when I'd gotten rid of my methadone, I hadn't had the flu. I'd been in withdrawal.[5] And while not getting addicted to narcotics might seem like a no brainer for you, it was a pretty big accomplishment for me.

Now, let's get back to the story at hand.

THE DAY BEFORE I LEFT, TIM CAME INTO THE TOWNHOUSE and said something cruel. I can no longer remember what it was—the words lost in a jumble of all the other mean words of our life together. What I do remember is that instead of keeping my mouth shut, I spat out, "Well, it doesn't matter because I'm leaving anyway."

Tim was halfway up the steps of our townhouse. He didn't yell or run or hit me. He just looked me straight in the eye and said, "Then I guess I'm just going to have to kill you, Laura." A fact, simply stated. As though he was commenting on the weather or a purchase from the store: "It looks like there will be rain on Tuesday, Laura." "I picked up milk on the way home, Laura." "I'm just going to have to kill you, Laura."

He didn't beat me or say anything else, just continued up the steps and went into our room. But the cards were on the table.

The next day I packed Phoebe into a cab. My car had been totaled by Tim several months ago, just a few days after he'd let the insurance run out. Did you catch that? My car—the one I'd loved with my all and everything, the one I'd started doing drugs for because I didn't want to leave my roommate sitting in it in the middle of the night—that car had been totaled by my drug-addict-drug-selling-abusive boyfriend. I guess doing that line with Peg didn't save it after all. So Phoebe and I took a cab—a cab full of everything I owned, and drove to the new apartment—an apartment with a security gate, a guard, and 24-hour surveillance. I'd paid for it with the money I'd sent home for my dad to save.

And now maybe you will begin to see that just as addictions came easy, so did a certain determination not to be completely destroyed. I hired a live-in nanny for Phoebe. It was easier than you might think. Free board in Hawaii was nothing to snub your nose at. Add in free food and all you really needed was a swim suit. Mary was nearly 6'2", blond, tomboyish, and kind.

Now everything was taken care of except me. Making the

wrong choices for myself was a gift of mine, but with Tim, I'd taken home the prize. Now it was time to right that wrong. At about the time I'd started dating Tim, another man had asked me out—repeatedly. His name, interestingly, was also Tim. I had had a choice between two Tims. One was an owner of a multi-national corporation that sold cars. He was nice-looking, rich, and kind. The other had just gotten out of jail, was much older than me, sold drugs for a living, and abused me almost to the point of death. Which one would you choose? Exactly. Which just goes to show that you weren't me. Because I picked Five-Star Loser Tim instead.

Me at age 28, Las Vegas

I HAD SPENT THE LAST YEAR AND A HALF REGRETTING THAT decision. The truth, if you want to hear it, is that I had spent the last six months thinking about Good Tim nearly every day, wondering how I could undo the decisions I'd made, and daydreaming about what my life would have been with Good Tim. I suppose I could have called him up when I'd been with Bad Tim, but on some level I understood that I had to pull myself up out of the sludge before I could jump into the pool. Bad Tim was dangerous. He would beat me up over tomatoes. Who knows what he might have done if I'd actually started calling another man and he'd found out.

But now Bad Tim was gone and I felt free to invite Good Tim into my life. Still, what was I supposed to do—call him up, tell him I was single, but now had a kid, a bad knee, and only a part-time job, then say, "Hey, so you wanna ask me out?" It didn't seem like a plan destined for success, but we've already discussed my decision-making skills, and I'd been thinking about him for so long that it just seemed best to know.

I didn't have his personal number, so I called him at work. I didn't think he'd be in town. If he was, I didn't think he'd pick up the phone. If he did, I didn't think he'd be single. And if he was, I really didn't think he'd be available to me. It's not the kind of thing that works if you think it through. Fortunately for me, I didn't.

Five days later, he and I were flying to Vancouver.

IT WASN'T A TRIP OF MOVING SLOW AND GETTING TO KNOW one another. It was a romantic whirlwind and I, happily, let myself be pulled in and blown away.

Good Tim—let's call him Timothy—was good to me, as I'd known he would be. In fact, as soon as we were established as a couple, I remember feeling that now Phoebe and I would be taken care of, now everything would be okay. And for a long time it was. For the next ten months I worked part time, got two more surgeries on my knee, and travelled with

Timothy. We went to Canada, Alaska, and Seattle. He bought me gifts. He bought Phoebe gifts. He bought my parents gifts. He bought Mary the nanny gifts. He had a room in his condo that was exclusively for gifts so that when he travelled on business he would have gifts to give the people he was working with.

If he was working late, and couldn't quite get off when I was ready to go out, he'd hand me a thousand dollars and tell me to go to the mall while he finished up. If I was on a trip with him and they were fishing and I was bored, he'd send me on a private plane with his secretary to go shopping.

Once when my nanny couldn't stay the week with Phoebe, he said, "Well, why don't I just fly Phoebe to your mom's house? I flew with Phoebe from Hawaii to Utah. Then Tim flew me to Seattle to meet him. He offered to send me to college. He tried to get me to take vitamins. He was always worried about my health and wanted me to stop drinking and smoking. It seemed like a relationship of ease and caring. It seemed like the type of story that should end with a wedding on a beach. It didn't.

I didn't want to be married, or even live with a man. I was determined not to be imprisoned by anyone the way I'd felt imprisoned with Tim. Not only that, but I didn't take any of Timothy's offers or advice. The best I did was hide my drug use from him so at least he didn't have to worry about that. Hiding my drug use was easier than you might think. At this point I only used cocaine recreationally—when I went to a club with a girlfriend, when I needed a pick-me-up, or wanted to drop a few pounds. And I didn't need any of those things when I was actually with Timothy. When we were together, it was a whirlwind, a romantic explosion of sexiness and kindness and closeness. But when we were apart, we were apart, almost as though it was a separate life. I should have known then, known that if we were living lives where a whole chunk of myself could be kept completely concealed, that this wasn't going to end well.

Yes, Timothy cared for me. Yes, he wanted to create a better life for me and Phoebe. And, yes, I cared about him. But neither of us had matured enough to take our relationship past the deep, sometimes co-dependent caring into the type of love that can last through any kind of turbulence. As a result, our story ended at an airport. In a bar. Naturally.

We'd been out of town for six days. I was eager to get back to my baby and sick of travelling. And then our flight got delayed. Timothy was Asian and, due to his travels and his job, he was carrying large amounts of currency from various countries. It looked suspicious. And my paperwork wasn't helping. As an air force brat, I had a Japanese birth certificate; and as someone who drank a lot, I had no driver's license. For the next several hours and maybe even days, we would be stuck in Vancouver. As soon as I found out, I went to the bar. And I didn't go slow. "Tequila please." After about eight shots of tequila, we still couldn't go through customs. I was going to miss Mother's Day with my daughter, and all Timothy could do was ask me why I was drinking in the middle of the day. I was drinking in the middle of the day because there was a problem, and when there were problems, I drank. It seemed simple enough. But I didn't say that. I doubt I even thought it. I was drunk. I was angry. I spat out, "I don't even know why we're together. You don't even like anything about me."

When they finally allowed us to fly the next day, we didn't sit together on the plane, didn't pick up our luggage together, didn't take the same cab home.

It was the end. Sometimes it surprises me that I didn't call him to apologize. Sometimes it surprises me that he didn't call to say he was disappointed it had played out like it had. But neither of us called. We must have both recognized the inevitable—it was over.

I went back to being a cocktail waitress. And Timothy went on with his life.

———————————————————

1. It is important to note that he never touched my pregnant stomach. My face was sufficient for his needs. If a person can be grateful for such a thing, then I am grateful.
2. Also, I knew that Tim would be gone when I got home. Every time he beat me, he would leave for several days after. He didn't want to face me, didn't want to see what he had done. I would have some time to regroup. Not to mention the fact that I was financially dependent on him and everything I owned was there—all of the baby clothes, everything. To leave that night would have left me with nothing.
3. Years later, I would find out from Tim's sisters that as a young child Tim had been horrifically abused. His father used to hang him upside down from a tree and would whip him without mercy—often for doing something small, like leaving his bike out. As Tim was being beaten, his sisters would be screaming, "Let him down. Let him down." He was the only boy in a sea of girls and he took the brunt of the punishment in his family.
4. Maybe they weren't really buying me diapers or food, but I wish I could tell them that they were buying me freedom—piece by piece. I wish I could thank them.
5. I consider it a tender mercy that, at the time, I thought my symptoms were the flu, not withdrawal. If I had known that I could fix myself by just taking another pill, I surely would have; and my relationship with opiates might have lasted longer than it did, becoming more complicated and entangled in my life. After all, that was the way I rolled.

CHAPTER FIVE

L eaving Timothy left me in a financially difficult
 situation. While it was true that I'd never asked
Timothy for money for anything, it seemed like he gave me
money for everything. When you show up in your boyfriend's
office and he hands you a thousand dollars to go spend at the
mall, it means that you just don't have a whole lot of worries
about money.

When you break up, it's easy to realize you've got rent to
pay and a daughter to raise. I had no car. I had my job at the
bar and that was something. But the corals in my knee were
constantly coming back. In seven years I had twelve surgeries. That made for a lot of lost work, lost money, and lost
mobility. I was paying for rent in Hawaii, food in Hawaii,
preschool in Hawaii, nannies in Hawaii. And let's not forget
the booze and drugs.

Along about this time, my mother sent my aunt who lived
in Hawaii, to spy out Tim's family and report back to her. She
came back with a glowing report of the extended family.
They were a big Polynesian family—nice people, church-

goers. Everyone (but me) agreed that my daughter should get to know them. They were her family too, her blood. They were her cousins, her aunts, her people. And they would rescue her occasionally from the humdrum life of a single mother who still partied, spoiled her child, and wouldn't keep a boyfriend even when the perfect one was staring her in the face. They didn't even know about the cocaine.

My mother and older brother both told me, "You can't hold it against them because of what Tim did. They're still her family. She deserves to get to know them."

The guilt needled me. It was true, after all. I was a single parent, and I knew that even though I loved Phoebe, my parenting usually came up woefully short. Maybe my daughter would benefit from more interaction with her cousins, her extended family. They really did seem nice. Once when I moved apartments, Tim's brother-in-law, William, brought over several men to help me. The job was done in a blink. They didn't ask for any money; they didn't ask for anything. I softened. I started getting to know Tim's sisters better. I even found that I liked them.

So I let Phoebe go with Tim's family. It wasn't much or often, but once every few months she'd spend the day at the beach, or go camping, or have a sleepover with her aunt, uncle, and cousins.

At first she liked it. And then she didn't. She began to beg me to stay, hide when one of her aunties came over to pick her up. Once, when I fell asleep on the couch while waiting for her relatives to arrive and take her for the weekend, she snuck out of our apartment and downstairs. The security guard brought her back up to me, and she repeated over and over, "I don't want to go. I don't want to go." But her aunt was already there to pick her up. She'd come all the way from the other side of the island. It felt impolite to say, "Oh sorry, we changed our minds." Besides, Aunt Polly always said, "Oh, it's just hard while *you're* here. As soon as she's there, she's fine."

Which made sense. Wasn't that how kids were? Wasn't that what kids do—cry when their moms are around and then act fine when they're gone? Yet in small, intangible ways Phoebe didn't seem fine. Once, while watching Phoebe leave —her dark, Cindy Brady pigtails bouncing against her shoulders, she turned and looked back at me—afraid, betrayed. It was a glance, a moment, something it seems like I should have forgotten. But I had a stack of those looks—seconds of my life that had begun to pile together in an uncomfortable way. Somehow they hung with me, haunting me in the moments I chose to think about them. I didn't know what to do about that, so I did the only thing besides using drugs that I knew to do. I called my mom. "Don't be rude," she scolded me. "They're just giving her good family values, not material possessions like you always do. You just spoil her and give her everything she wants and then because they don't, she doesn't want to go."

And the thing was, I did spoil her. I did give her too many possessions. And I didn't give her enough of what she needed —time and mothering and family. But I did love her—loved her like the sun, loved her like I've never loved anything before or since. That nudge of uncomfortable intuition nagged at me as I continued to send her to be with her aunt and uncle. Nagged at me until I—or my mother or my brother —pushed it away. Didn't it seem better to let her interact with her family, didn't it seem better that someone else could help —give her outings and cousins and fresh air and rowdy children's play. Wasn't I just being short-sighted, selfish?

It certainly seemed plausible. I was sometimes selfish, often short-sighted. So I ignored my gut. And Phoebe continued to spend nights and days, on and off for the next two years, with her extended family.

Glamour shot! Me with Phoebe, age 4

CHAPTER SIX

I n the meantime, I was partying harder again. I was still young, still pretty, still fascinated by money and clothes and things, still drawn to the high, fun life that was there in Hawaii for the living.

I wasn't dating any one guy, but there were a few I hung out with regularly. Mario was one of them. He was an investor and a gambler and apparently good at both. He spoiled me with jewelry and clothes. Once he bought me a half carat diamond—like another guy might have bought roses with a little card stuck into them that said, "Just because." That's the kind of money Mario tossed around.

Mario drove me home one night and we were sitting around having a few drinks when Tim called. I don't know how he got my number, but when I answered the phone he said, "I know you're there and I know who you're with." I hadn't heard from Tim for over a year and suddenly I felt like he was standing right outside of my apartment, peering in.

Mario knew Tim a little. They had crossed paths at bars and after hours "casinos." As soon as Tim called, Mario left.

He said he couldn't take it; too much drama. I think he was afraid. The truth is that he had plenty of reasons for that.

The full details of Tim's life and past were and still are somewhat unknown to me. What I know for sure is this. Tim's "job" was not just selling drugs, but also acting as a Hawaiian syndicate—a type of Hawaiian mob boss who gets payments from businesses for keeping them "safe," which really just means that if you pay they don't come in and tear the place apart. All those times we'd go to a club and people would smile and wave, the crowd parting so Tim could go through—I had thought it was because Tim was likeable, loved, respected. It wasn't. In reality Tim was feared, cowed to, and paid. After we broke up, I started to hear stories of the Tim I didn't know before we got together. This Tim would go into a bar and if they wouldn't change the TV channel, he would pick up the TV and throw it across the room.

So I couldn't blame Mario for being afraid. I was too. I was twenty-seven years old. I had a baby, no education, no job that would lead me to someplace better. Then this guy who I'd tried to shake out of my life had dropped back in. I was troubled by how easily he'd gotten my number, troubled by how quickly he'd scared my date away, troubled that Tim seemed determined to keep coming back, determined to ruin any little pieces of me he could. Plus, I was drunk.

That night when Tim called I felt trapped in my own house, in my own life just as much as I'd felt trapped in the room I'd shared with him. That night there didn't seem to be an apartment distant enough, an island wide enough to run away. There was no place to go to escape him. It felt like all of the doors in my short life had suddenly clicked shut and locked tight.

That night, in addition to Remi Martin, cigarettes, and a line, I pounded Valium, Quaaludes, Halcyon, and Percocet into my 5'4," 120 pound frame. It was a fantastic overdose that I hoped would take me someplace better. I knew heaven was a long shot, but I was hoping for a decent little purgatory. Instead, I landed in the ER where they pumped as much as they could out of my gut. When I woke up, it was with a nurse beside my bed and a cop outside my door.

I had no idea how I'd gotten there, although later I would learn that I had called my mother and told her I was sorry, but I just couldn't do it anymore[1]. She had called 911 and they had come and found me unconscious. But I didn't remember any of this. I just woke up in a hospital, hooked up to an IV, feeling like brimstone had been pumped into my belly. I would be escorted to the state mental hospital for a 72-hour evaluation. I told the nurse I wanted to leave, that I was going to leave, that this had all been a big mistake. She didn't argue with the mistake part, but instead of letting me get my things and go, she had the cop come in and handcuff me to the bed[2].

The psychiatric hospital—the one for people without insurance—was on the other side of the island—an hour and a half away. I was taken there in an ambulance, handcuffed to the gurney for the duration of the drive. As we drove I felt like I was on the set of a horror movie. The landscape got less and less civilized—fewer houses and shops, more vegetation, darker roads. It was an empty little piece of looney bin out in the middle of nowhere.

The horror movie didn't end when I was taken through the doors. The next seven years of my life I would find myself in jails, slums, locked cars, and bare apartments. I would be held against my will. I would have my body probed by addicts. I would have a gun held to my head in a locked blue van. But the scariest place I've been was that institution.

Everything in the institution was completely white. Or, rather, everything had once been white, and it was still trying to, but failing. The beds had no pillows. The blanket and sheet (just one) were torn with holes and they smelled like bleach. Under the blankets was a plastic mattress that was cracked, the stuffing pushing out of it with smells of cleaning solvent and funk.

I had a small, steel toilet in my room with no lid or any other detachable parts, due to the institution's fear that people would use them as weapons against themselves or anyone else. Any and all mirrors were made of plastic, and the toilet paper was thin enough that I could see through it. When we ate, we went to a large eating hall. Picnic tables were bolted to the floor and we were not allowed to have forks or knives, only plastic spoons. After the meal was over, the spoons were counted. If one was missing, the staff searched floors, benches, trays. If it still couldn't be located, they searched the people until the spoon was found.

The only windows in the building were extremely narrow and high up—almost to the ceiling, so that residents couldn't crawl through and escape. But they were always open. When it was cold and dank outside it was cold and dank inside. Trade winds came through the thick screens and the wind howled through those vents like ghost hounds.

Maybe I could have gotten over the fact that everything smelled like it'd been peed on and then sterilized, maybe I could have dealt with the fact that I was forced to eat like an angry two-year-old, maybe I could have handled the dark, damp, whistling windows if it wasn't for the fact that we were all together: schizophrenics, cutters, compulsive people, near-comatose people, suicidal people—the obsessive, the afraid, the screamers, the sulkers. There was no division or separation. None of the doors locked during the day, except the front doors that penned us in. If someone with eight personalities or an obsessive compulsive need to touch everything wanted to walk into my room in the middle of the day, he or she certainly could.

It was like the state mental hospital had been designed by Satan himself.

You didn't get to say, "Oh, I don't belong here."

You didn't get to say, "He's crazier than me."

You didn't get to say, "This is my space; I don't want that woman here."

We were all equals, without rights, tied together—desperate to walk away but without the ability to do so. A perfect little hell on earth.

That first day I didn't come out of my room. And then, that night, the screaming started—residents howling and moaning. It echoed through the building, carried through the windows where the wind took the sounds into the mountains that surrounded the institution and then spun them back towards us so that it seemed voices were crying through the hills.

Even now, I would choose an army of gangsters with guns over that place.

Each day a friend came to visit me, tried to vouch for me, told them he'd keep an eye on me and keep me safe. And every day that friend came and told me, "You can't leave; they won't let you." Seventy-two hours was how long I was supposed to stay and seventy-two hours was how long I stayed. It was good the windows were high and narrow. Otherwise, I would have clawed my way up until my fingernails ripped off just to get out. We all would have.

WHEN I GOT BACK HOME, I HAD SOME THINGS TO SORT OUT. I'd never actually told my parents why I wouldn't marry Tim. Now I did. They had assumed, I think, that I was just irresponsible, making crappy choices and getting knocked up. That was only mostly true. After my stint at the mental institution, it was time to come clean. *Dear Mom and Dad, The reason I didn't marry Tim is because if I did he would have eventually beat me to death. I'm still afraid he will.*

When I called my dad and told him, he went nuts. As soon as he got off the phone with me, he called the police department in Hawaii. "I need to talk to a detective," he said. He told them about Tim, the threats, and then he said, "My name is Donald R. Findlay. This is my address. I'm going to tell you right now, if this SOB lays a hand on my daughter or threatens her in anyway, I'm going to come over and kill him. You don't even have to ask who killed the SOB because it was me. My name is Findlay, and I've been through two wars. I've had a full life. I'm not going to have my daughter live in fear. If you find him dead, you don't need to look for anybody else. It was me."

The last four years had been hard—my knee was a mess, my love life was a piece of ugly modern art with the ups and downs in all the wrong places, money was tight, I had a little girl to care for and I didn't really know how. Often—so often —I'd spent the last few years feeling like I was just going it alone. I hadn't told my parents much because I knew I was screwing things up and I knew they would know, and I knew they would be disappointed. And I hated that—hated feeling that I was always the difficult child, the girl who gave them more grief than all three boys combined, hated that I knew there were things they would change about me if they could. My parents, after all, were only human with struggles of their own. By this point, they had divorced each other and were married to new spouses. They were often wishing I would go to college, get a different job, settle down with someone nice, be a different version of me.

It was good to know that sometimes that didn't matter. It was good to know that my parents still loved me enough to stand up for me, to stick their necks out for me, to act a little crazy every once in a while. I appreciated that.

For whatever reason, after my dad called, Tim left me alone.

AND THEN I FELL IN LOVE FOR REAL.

I met Rod, as I met most of the men I dated, at the bar where I worked. Rod was a two beers kind of man, but he'd come in with friends and we'd had an instant connection, a vibe, an intense chemistry. We started off well, hit some serious rocks, and then started over again. When we did, I began to see that even better than that chemistry was that Ron knew my weaknesses and loved me anyway. He knew about my past, my drug use, my knee, my everything. He'd seen me at my weakest. He'd already learned to forgive me. He looked past the flaws into the me that I was and still loved me. Up to that point, I'm not sure I'd experienced anything like that from a man I'd dated.

Before, with Tim, I had had chemistry, and he'd seen me at my freest and my lowest. At the end of the day all of that chemistry and intimacy had gotten me was abuse and mistreatment.

And then later, Timothy had known parts of me (the best ones I tried to show him), and he had treated me well. We hadn't had an intense chemistry, but we had shared a mutual infatuation, a deep caring, and some sort of co-dependence where I gave him someone to dote on and he gave me someone who made me feel safe.

Now, Rod somehow combined chemistry with the knowledge of me into a deep, work-a-day love. We were together all the time when we weren't at our jobs. Our dating was both more ordinary and yet more intimate than anything I'd experienced before. Rod would make me dinner and we would eat together. Or he'd pick me up from work. Or he'd be waiting for me in bed when I got home at two in the morning.

Phoebe was often with us, and she adored Rod. He took her trick-or-treating, cared for her during and after my knee surgeries, and loved her. He pitched in and drove her around and worked hard. Every other weekend his two boys would come and we would all eat and relax and enjoy ourselves in an almost boringly normal way.

My mother thought Rod was the moon and stars. She would have dragged me to the altar herself if she could have. My brother Randy moved to Hawaii, and when he did, he became good friends with Rod. My family loved him. I loved him. It seemed like there was nothing to stop us, or even slow us down. But I always found a way.

The first time Rod proposed, he didn't pop out a ring and fall to one knee. The first time he proposed, he said, "I don't want you to have to work anymore. I want to take care of you and Phoebe. I'll be a really good stepfather." That was all true. But I told him I couldn't do it. He would be amazing, but I was terrified to live with someone again after what had happened with Tim. Even though I didn't always love working, even though my knee made working painful some of the time, even though the hours were odd and often difficult, I was afraid to step away from work, to step into a household role, to do the things that had allowed Tim to hold me down. It wasn't that I thought Rod would do those things too. It was just fear—primal, simple, irrational, but still very real.

Rod understood at first. He gave me space. He wanted me to be able to work through the feelings and heal from the scars that Tim had left when he'd locked me into a life where my only cord to the outside world was one he held around my neck.

Even so, every few months, sometimes even weeks, Rod would repeat his proposal. He always wanted me to move in with him. He asked me to marry him repeatedly. Besides the fact that we were crazy in love, it would have made financial sense. We were renting two apartments, juggling two budgets. And we were kind of a family already. We slept over at each other's houses every single night. I would bring Phoebe when I went to Rod's house. And she would sleep on the fold-out couch in the living room. Which she hated because she was terrified of sleeping alone. So she would often come into our bedroom and sleep with me on my side of the bed or put blankets on the floor and sleep there. Ron and I even argued like regular parents over this fact. He thought I was being a pushover, but I could tell that—for whatever reasons— Phoebe was deeply scared of sleeping in a room by herself. And for all his arguing about sleeping arrangements, Rod loved Phoebe like his own child. It felt like old married people stuff. Except when it didn't.

As the months wore on, Rod began to wonder why I still wouldn't marry him. He felt that it should be obvious to me that he wasn't going to trap me in my own house, or abuse me to the point of hospitalization, or anything else remotely awful. And it *was* obvious. But I still wasn't ready to settle down. Besides being terrified of losing my place in my own life the way I felt I had with Tim, I was also terrified of settling down and missing out on the exciting life that Hawaii had to offer, a life that would move on without me if I stepped away from it.

I had always, even from a young age, been interested in glamour and beauty, excitement and intrigue.[3] I wanted to have the freedom and money to be where the action was. I wanted the exhilaration of nightclubs and fast living. I wanted the comfort and glamour of money I could throw into clothes and beautiful cars.

The truth was that, with the lifestyle I'd always envisioned for myself, Rod just seemed so broke. Yeah, you heard me. My problem with my perfectly wonderful boyfriend was that his perfectly decent and respectable job made me feel poor. Rod had a middle-class job, child support to pay, and he drove an old beat up car. It didn't fit with the bedazzled life I'd planned for myself. After crazy abusive Tim, I longed for a measure of financial comfort. After rich Timothy, I expected it.

But that wasn't our only problem. In addition to desperately trying to maintain my independence while also adjusting my expectations to something somewhat reasonable, there were technical difficulties to our relationship. Our work hours didn't line up. He needed to be up for work and sharp by eight. I didn't get home till two or three in the morning. If he waited up, he was exhausted the next day.

Beyond that, Rod knew how much I still liked to party. He knew I did drugs and he knew I drank a lot. Most of the time, he was still too in love for it to bother him. Still, it seeped in—my addictions, my dependence—connecting little problems to big insecurities or big problems to little insecurities. To me, my habits didn't seem like addiction or dependence. All I wanted, I told myself, was to keep working, to keep my independence, to keep having fun, to not get stuck at home again.

What I didn't tell myself, but what is easy to see when I look back, was that one of the reasons working as a cocktail waitress remained so important to me was that at work I could do a line, at work I could get high. At work I could be with friends who also liked to get high. And Rod wasn't part of this world. But other men were. Players, partyers, movers, gamblers. They had hot cars and fast ways. They were people who got high, people who rolled high. Because of this, when I was at work, Rod always felt a little insecure, an outsider who didn't want to come in, but really wished I would come out.

Despite the fact that Rod knew about my drug use, I never used drugs around him. The closest I ever came—and I only did this a few times when I was desperate—was to go into his bathroom and do a line. As far as I know, he didn't know that I ever did this. Even so, everything was starting to get to Rod. He was exhausted—physically from waiting for me to get home and climb into bed with him (he was still in love enough to wait), and mentally from my refusal to settle down with him, commit long-term to him, trust him, and let him trust me.

One night when I came home from work, Rod was in bed in tears. "I can't handle this," he told me. "I'm screwing up at work. I'm tired all the time. I just want you to marry me. I want to take care of you and Phoebe. I just want a normal life."

The problem was that I didn't. Not just yet anyway. So if he could just wait a little, maybe a lot longer, then maybe I'd be ready.

And then, one night, a friend gave me a ride home from work. He was Japanese, decent-looking, and he came to the club a lot. He drove a hot red Porsche. That Porsche sat in the parking spot of my apartment all night long and when my brother saw it, he called Rod and told him—ratted me out just like we were kids again. Unbeknownst to my brother, he ratted me out for all the wrong reasons. It was true that red Porsche guy had stayed all night—stayed all night doing lines on my coffee table with me. Nothing else. But I couldn't tell my brother that. He didn't know I did drugs at all. Even without knowing that, he hated the lifestyle I was living—the bars and booze and cigarettes. I couldn't tell him that I'd picked up another awesome habit. So I didn't. I told him the guy had come over, had a couple drinks and then was too drunk to drive home so he'd stayed the night. My brother didn't believe me. Neither did Rod.

Rod called me crying, saying he couldn't do it anymore, saying he was going to have a nervous breakdown, worrying about who I was with, what I was doing, stressing that I wanted to be out partying instead of home with him. He said he was exhausted, that it was messing with him and affecting his job. He couldn't trust what I said, believe who he thought I was.

I thought he would come around, begged him to come around. But it was over—one more thing to add to the list of wonderful things lost.

---

1. I do not remember calling my mother at all, but I had. My mother would later tell me that I had called her asking that she would take care of Phoebe for me. I knew that Phoebe didn't deserve any of this. I was already drunk enough that my memory would black out the conversation, but I told my mom that I loved my family; I just didn't feel like I could make a life for myself with the constant threat of Tim.

2. This sounds cruel, but it is actually standard procedure with people who are a threat to themselves.

3. Even at age thirteen, I'd gotten myself a job babysitting so I could buy fashionable clothes.

PART II
SAN DIEGO

CHAPTER SEVEN

I t was one thing too many. After twelve years in Hawaii I was ready for a new start. Two friends were visiting from San Diego. They told me I should come. Six months later, I was there. I had just finished my twelfth and final knee surgery. The doctor had given up on attacking the corals as they grew. Instead, he opened my knee up completely and scraped it out, removing any abscesses he could. After that, the problems stopped.

I felt like a new woman. I was ready to be a new woman. For the first time in eight years I was ready to give up drugs —not just put them away for a pregnancy or ignore them while I was visiting my parents or on a trip with my boyfriend. For the first time since I'd started using cocaine, I was ready to be *done*. And for the first time in eight years, I was in a place where I felt like I could be done. The old friends and familiar clubs were gone. A door had opened for a brand new me to walk through. And I did.

For about five months I didn't do any drugs. In fact, I barely drank because alcohol and cocaine were so bound together for me that I couldn't give up one without the other. I missed the drugs. But more than that I was glad to be away from them. It wasn't easy. My stomach felt weird; I was always hungry, constantly tired. And I was gaining weight. That was the worst part. I'd always used cocaine as a sort of diet pill. It sped up my metabolism to the point that I was thin when I was using it. I could eat what I wanted; I could drink what I wanted. If I put on a few pounds, I'd do some lines and the extra weight would melt away like I'd just consumed a miracle skinny tonic. Now, even though I was still a healthy body weight by normal standards, I felt heavy and lumpy.

My dad and stepmom came to visit and I'd put on maybe twenty pounds since the last time my dad saw me in Hawaii. It seems important to point out that this only brought me up to about 145 pounds, a tiny tip into barely chubby. But in Hawaii, I'd always looked thin and amazing—the movie star child he wanted me to be. Now he felt like I was letting myself go, slipping. He didn't know that my slipping was really a huge step back into a healthy life. He didn't know that the reason I'd always stayed so thin in Hawaii was because I was using cocaine. He didn't know what a sacrifice it was for me to give up a bit of my figure to reclaim a bit of my life. All he knew was that he couldn't stand to see me packing on the pounds. He offered to buy me a new wardrobe worth of clothes if I got my figure back. He told me, "I just want my beautiful little girl back." The message—accidental though it may have been—was clear. He wanted the old me back. She was cuter, more deserving than this new slob I'd become. His disapproval of my appearance wasn't exactly the most heartening development in my new drug-free life.

But his disapproval of my parenting was worse.

To be fair, Phoebe was swinging out of control. She was

six years old. While my dad was visiting she refused to sleep in her room. If I tried to make her, she wouldn't sleep at all, so usually I'd let her come into my room. She also wouldn't let anyone turn off the light in her bedroom. Ever. Phoebe had always been sassy. Now she was worse—hot and cold all the time—sometimes mean to kids, vicious even, sometimes sweet as honey, tender. It was common for her to have outbursts—in kindergarten she had stabbed a kid in the hand with her pencil. It was common for her to be angry, and she didn't discriminate—both children and adults could be the targets of her wrath. Even as a toddler, it had been difficult to control her. Now, it seemed impossible. Because of this, I let her get her way with a bunch of stuff. And when I did, my family would say, "You let her get her own way all the time; that's why she's acting like this."

Which I couldn't deny. It seemed like one more thing I just couldn't get right.

And then it happened. One night after my dad left, Phoebe stayed at a friend's house and I was home alone for the night. It had just been so draining—the move, my recovering knee, the fact that I still missed Rod so much that I felt sick to my stomach every time I saw a couple holding hands. And then there was my dad's lack of approval for the way I looked, for the way I was raising my daughter. I just wanted a drink—a nice simple drink. No, that's not true. I just wanted to get ripped. And I did. The thing was I couldn't just get plastered without also getting high. They were like cookies and milk for me.

I asked my friend if he knew where I could go to get some cocaine. I don't remember if he argued with me, if he told me it was a bad idea. It doesn't matter because in the end he took me to a sketchy area downtown—the proverbial dark alley. A

Mexican guy was standing on the street—just like he would in a bad B movie. "Ask him," my friend said. And it was as simple as that. This was the drug area. It was the middle of the night.

"Do you have any coke," I asked, like I was bumming a match for my cigarette.

"I don't have any coke," he said, "but I've got crystal."

I didn't know what crystal was, had never even heard of methamphetamines, but it was a white powder. And that would do.

"You'll like it," the dealer said to me. "It's like coke, but better."

And it was. Higher, more alert. I didn't eat for hours, I didn't eat for days.

The Mexican dealer gave me his number, told me to call if I ever needed anything else; he'd hook me up.

But of course I wouldn't do that. I was sober now. Well, mostly. This had just been a little blip, a slip. I went home, sobered up, went back to being drug free. See, I was fine. I was totally under control. I'd just gotten drunk; the drugs had been an accident. I wasn't planning to do it again. But the thing was—now I knew there was a different kind of drug out there, a powerful drug, another way I could lose myself. If I ever needed to. But I didn't. Because of course I had every-thing under control.

Like that I didn't have a job. Couldn't get a job because my knee was still recovering and intensely weak from years of surgery. I couldn't stand for long periods of time, which meant I couldn't be a waitress or a bartender, or even be a gas station attendant.

Like that my daughter was crazy out-of-control and getting crazier every day. I had to take the mirrors off the doors in my apartment because I was worried Phoebe would hurt herself by smashing them off—accidentally or on purpose.

Like that it was just me and her and we were both trying, but both still a wreck. Which kind of seemed worse than not trying at all.

AND THEN ONE DAY MY NEIGHBOR—A WOMAN SEVERAL years older than me, the mother of a friend, came up to me and said, "I know you don't want to hear this, but I think something happened to your daughter." The "something" she meant was sinister, bad—something that shouldn't have happened to a little girl, but sometimes did.

I don't remember why she came up to talk to me. I don't remember if we were already talking, if I'd vented to her about Phoebe's behavior. I do remember that there was a laundry in between both of our apartments so we passed each other frequently. I do remember that she told me, "You need to go get her checked out."

"Believe me," I said. "Nothing's happened."

"Believe me," she said. "You should go get her checked out."

Whatever. I knew Phoebe had never been molested. She had spent most of her life around me and her female nannies whom I trusted.

My neighbor shrugged. "Just ask her," she said.

Fine. I would. I asked her the next day. "Did anyone ever touch you in your privates?"

"No," she said.

Great. Good.

Except that it wasn't. Even I could tell. Phoebe looked down when she said it, shifty eyes as though a secret had been uncovered. I hadn't made a big deal out of it or introduced it as an embarrassing topic. Just a simple question. A simple question with a simple answer that didn't feel simple at all. Still, I didn't press her, didn't cross examine.

Then two weeks later, heading to the car wash with our yellow Mazda, the sunroof open, Phoebe started screaming—hysterical, choking sobs. I thought a bee had flown in through the sun roof. I thought she'd been stung. Until she spoke. "You're right, you're right. It was Papa Tong[1], Mommy. He told me he'd kill me if I ever told, kill me, and you too."

AND THEN MY LIFE SPINNING SPINNING SPINNING. SO OUT-OF-control. So wrong in every way. I was sick to my stomach and mad as hell. All those trips across the island, her resistance to going, her fear of being alone in bed, her hysteria when someone woke her up—it all clicked into place—the way her Uncle Tong would come to her in the night when she visited, take her from her bed, steal her from herself.

I've been through so much in the years of my life, broken so many laws, made so many mistakes, tasted consequence after consequence, but there is only one thing I feel I'll never quite recover from—and letting my daughter into the clutches of that horrible man is it.

Looking back, it's possible to see there were so many other ways to handle this news—so many other things I could have tried, said, done to help my daughter, to heal the situation, to recover. But I only knew one way to deal with trouble, especially trouble as deep, as painful, as regret-filled as this.

IT WAS A REMORSE I TRIED TO WASH AWAY WITH DRINK, BUT it wouldn't be washed away. Night after night I had tequila,

Chivas Regal, vodka. Night after night Phoebe, with her young, hurt, troubled mind saw me not coping or helping her cope, but tipsy, drunk. Perhaps you can guess that this didn't help her much, didn't make her feel more secure or steady.

The more my behavior deteriorated, the worse Phoebe became. We were two celestial bodies orbiting a dying sun, about to implode. I couldn't comfort her because I couldn't explain to her that I had let her get harmed, that I had tossed her into the arms of that evil man. I certainly couldn't explain to her that my mother and brother had thrown their support behind the unknown Polynesian family, instead of standing behind me. And that, in doing so, they'd pressed and pressured me to make Phoebe go, telling me my own parenting was insufficient, and that that nice, big church-going family would certainly make everything right. I couldn't tell my daughter that I was furious beyond words at my own family for not standing in my court, no matter how much of a loser it looked like I would turn out to be. What had I done? Given my daughter too many things, spoiled her, left her with nannies while I went to get high? It wasn't great parenting; it was terrible. But what had they done—pressured me to ignore my instincts, to ignore my daughter, to turn away from each hurt, terrified look she gave me when she didn't want to go. The emotion was too confusing, too intense. I wanted my feelings to swim away in the river of whiskey that I fed it. And sometimes they did. But never for long.

I called the police in Hawaii, told them to arrest William Tong, told them what he'd done to my child (as well as two of her cousins, and possibly countless other children). They checked in on it, told me that they couldn't see that anything was going on. That made me feel even more helpless and betrayed.

Years later, talking to one of Phoebe's other aunts, she

would tell me, "Oh, there have been rumors of that for years."
I wanted to punch her in the face, wanted to drown her in my
own years of sorrow.

---

1. Her uncle—Tim's sister's husband, who had been so "helpful" to me
all those years in Hawaii.

CHAPTER EIGHT

I t didn't take long to be back on drugs.
I called the street corner dealer—his name was José—
and he hooked me up, easy as that.

Phoebe ran through the neighborhood with a butcher knife, threatening to kill herself. Six years old.

I called the police, not knowing what to do. They told me to bring her to a psychiatric facility. "Just come over and check it out." But what they really meant was, *Just come over and check her in.* As soon as I told the psychiatrist what Phoebe had done, he said Phoebe had to stay. One month. The law required it; she was a danger to others and herself.

It was the first time my baby would be physically taken away from me. It wouldn't be the last.

I visited her every day in the institution. I visited her so much and so regularly that the staff decided to give me my own visiting hours. Most of the children were not visited regularly, and it was hard for those kids to see me showing up every day for my daughter when they hadn't had a visit all week. So now I showed up at my own special time. Sometimes I was a little high, sometimes I was drunk and then high to take care of the drunk. But I was always there for that horrible month they kept her. They gave her counseling, put her on meds. And, eventually, sent her home.

It didn't help. I guess I can't say I blame them, though I still kind of want to. It's always difficult to help a child who's been through what my child went through. But it's much more difficult to help a child who's been through what my child went through when the child's parent cannot even help herself. And I couldn't.

ABOUT A MONTH AFTER BUYING FROM JOSÉ, HE GOT BUSTED. I couldn't believe it. I'd never had a drug friend go to jail. It took away my supplier and forced me to look somewhere else for my high. When I asked a friend where I could find some meth, she rattled off several names of people willing to get me some drug if I would *kick them down*. I'd never even heard the phrase before. In Hawaii, there were just serious drug dealers—none of the small-time, back porch dealers that San Diego had to offer.

To get *kicked down* meant that a person would both get your drug and deliver your drug, but you had to "pay" them a few lines. So they assumed all the risk in exchange for a measly high. It was what addicts did when they didn't have enough money to buy, but really needed their drugs.

I thought it was fantastically stupid. If they were going to risk being caught and jailed as dealers, then they should be actual dealers, with the money and benefits that dealers enjoyed. I mean, I knew that if I was going to take a risk, I was going to take a *risk*.

It was just the smallest snatch of an idea—the thought that there might be some risks worth taking if the potential payoff was high enough. For now, I figured I could find my drug without employing half the city of San Diego as my delivery guys. And I did.

José called me collect from jail and told me he had a favor to ask me—a big favor. I might have been a messed up methhead who was losing control of her one precious child, but I was still—had always been—eager to help others. I tried to be generous. It was the one thing I could lean on when my life got tough.

José told me he'd been arrested and that he needed me to help him talk to his family. His wife couldn't accept collect calls; and that was the only type of call you could make from jail. José would need me to set my phone up so it would take three-way calls. To do this I had to call my phone company and make a change. After I did, he would call me collect, I would accept the charges, and then he would be able to talk to his family through the three-way call.

The truth is that even though this was inconvenient and even expensive, I would have done it for him for free, for nothing. But he offered me something. If I did this for him, he would call his suppliers and hook me up. That seemed fair enough. After all, I wouldn't be able to get drugs from him anymore. It seemed nice that he would give me the number of his people so I could still get my drugs. Like your hairdresser offering you a back-up when she goes out of town.

I was trying to help him out; he was trying to help me out. Both of us were misguided—our sense of generosity, of right and wrong oddly misplaced. And yet still there. Even in a crappy life, even in a circle of drug sellers and addicts, good people were there—helping in all the wrong ways maybe, but trying to help nonetheless.

After José talked to his family, we did a three-way call with his supplier. He told them I was cool. I thought I was getting a new drug guy. What I was really getting was a direct contact to the Mexican drug cartel. When I showed up at Rafael's house, he had a locked gate for a front door, an enormous pit bull, and a bunch of guys hanging around a table with triple beam scales for weighing drugs, hand guns casually tucked away. That day, instead of getting my usual fix, I got four hundred dollars worth of crystal meth on credit. It's like getting a product wholesale. You can get high for free, and sell the rest at retail. Which meant I would make money. For selling people drugs.

You're following, right? In that simple transaction, I slipped from user to seller, from passive to active, from poor to rich, from loser to destroyer. I made a thousand bucks from the drugs sold from that first transaction. When I brought Rafael back his four hundred dollars, he gave me more meth to use and sell. We were partners now, working the market from different angles.

Looking back, I realize how lucky I was—a small white woman in a band of Mexican drug dealers, picking up my drug from a barred-off house in an area of town where I often couldn't leave right away because of a shooting going on in the neighborhood.

The men who gave me my drugs watched over me like brothers and I always felt safe with them. Yet, it's easy to see that it didn't have to be that way. They could have raped me or kidnapped me or taken me and sold me into human trafficking. As it was, the things that made me so vulnerable— my gender, my race, my lack of Spanish—also made me a valuable asset to them. They knew I would sell to my white friends, expand their circle, bring a lot of new money to their door. And I did. It was easy.

· · ·

Or rather it looked easy, started easy. It fell into my hands, and then I made a lot of money. Quickly.

Every person who becomes an addict is going to need something to sell.

For women, that usually means they end up selling their bodies. Other times people will burglarize houses and steal from stores, or even friends and family, then sell those goods.

In that way, dealing seemed downright moral. I wouldn't have to steal anything. I never even had to think about prostitution. Dealing seemed like the cleanest act in town. Never mind that people who did steal were always offering me their stuff in exchange for drugs. Never mind that I often took it, knowing full well that it was stolen.

Over the years I got toys for Phoebe, Super Nintendos, electronics, leather outfits, even a chinchilla fur coat. I got cars, including a white Triumph Spitfire convertible. If I'd wanted, I could have gotten credit cards. Users and gang members just kept the hot items at their houses. I'd go to a house around eleven at night since I couldn't do much else then.[1] I should have been sleeping, but I wasn't; and I couldn't go out because I didn't want to get noticed by the cops. So I'd get high and go shopping in my customers' houses, sifting through the troves of stolen items they were willing to give me for my drugs. I could have had anything at all that I wanted, because the thing I had was something they wanted more.

The people who had been burglarized never crossed my mind. After all, it wasn't like I had personally stolen anything. In fact, I used to tell people I was an honest criminal. The addicts buying drugs were going to steal no matter what. I figured I might as well benefit. It was a mantra I repeated to myself throughout my years as a drug user and dealer. I considered using harmless, even beneficial in its way since it was all I could do to relieve my sadness. Because of this, it became difficult to see the compromising actions of others who were also addicted. We weren't trying to hurt anyone, I reasoned. We were just trying not to hurt so much ourselves.

And we all had morals of one type or another—things we wouldn't do that made us feel we hadn't slipped as low as that other guy—that other guy who would do *anything*. That wasn't us, we told ourselves, clinging to tiny rules as lives shattered around us. *Oh, I never smoke the stuff; it's terrible for your lungs*. Or *I only smoke it so I don't destroy my veins*. Or *I just shoot it; that's the purest way—no damage to my lungs or nose*.

We all had the best way, the safest way—the highest road as we trudged our way to hell through the bottom of a swamp. As for me, I never sold to first time users, never tried to get anyone hooked. If someone already used, I figured they might as well do business with me, since they were going to get their fix somewhere anyway. But if someone was just naïve or curious, I swatted them away. "No way," I'd say. "You're not getting involved with this crap."

I'd done this with my own little brother when I'd lived in Hawaii. He'd visited and begged me to let him try coke, just a taste, just a touch. He wanted to understand the experience, the high. No way. I would never let him even hold the stuff that I knew was tightening its chalky grip on me.

In this type of way, we all held to the morals that seemed so small as to be practically invisible to an outsider. We gripped them with all the fervor of a drowning sailor. Occasionally, you'd see someone let go, watch them sink into the abyss. These were the users in ditches and gutters. These were the users with children who starved and dogs who slept in their own feces. The rest of us held on; and though it didn't always look like it mattered, I believe it still did.

Sometimes I wonder if my refusal to sell to first time users—my tiny little standard—kept my head above the water enough to maintain a piece of my humanity, enough so that when the time came, when I was ready and desperate, I wouldn't be totally drowned.

———————————————

1. Between 11:00 PM and 4:30 AM was what we called *jack up time*—the time when the cops were out, ready to pull anybody over who gave them a funny look.

CHAPTER NINE

W hen you do drugs, you always have friends. You have friends coming out of your high little ears. We did drugs together, got referrals for dealers from each other, lied for each other—you know, relationship-building stuff.

When you deal drugs, you also have money. Tons of money. I was shopping every day, buying cute clothes for me and Phoebe. It was so much easier, so much nicer than living off the government dole like we'd been doing. I was going to do drugs and drink alcohol anyway, so what was the problem with using it to create a better life for me and my daughter?

As the money and friends kept rolling in, it became even harder for me to see the harm in anything I was doing. I didn't worry that my friends would turn on me or get me into trouble. How could they? These were the people who were begging to be my roommates, offering really cheap rent, happy to babysit my daughter when I had work to do. And I didn't think for a second that I could lose my daughter over it. At the time I thought that children only got taken away from their parents if they'd been physically abused. I wasn't doing anything even remotely close to physical abuse. I was buying

Phoebe nice clothes, expensive shoes, any toy she asked for. And while all these great-seeming things were happening, I was also taking care of my problems. I didn't want to think about my past, about my failed relationships, about Phoebe's abuse, about anything uncomfortable at all. So I didn't. The drugs made that all go away. And when the high wore off, I still had the money to enjoy.

Which was the great thing about dealing. I got three highs for the price of one. Drugs made me numb. But they also made me rich. And being rich made me feel powerful, successful. For the first time in my life, I felt like I was really good at something. I was respected in the drug community. I was needed. Which was its own kind of drug, its own kind of new release, and soon enough its own sweet addiction. Later, when I finally cleaned up, giving up the drugs was hard, giving up the money was harder, and starting anew as a failure was the hardest of all.

Plus, we all know money can buy happiness, right? Stability. Joy. And health. Let's not forget our health.

THE NIGHT I BROKE MY LEG, I WAS WITH FRIENDS. GOOD friends, friends who were dating each other. Jim was sleeping, coming down off a high. I was with his girlfriend, Cindy, and two other guys. It was a one bedroom apartment with an open kitchen area. We were sitting there on bar stools around the counter, chopping lines on a plate. Cindy and one of the guys were smoking it in a pipe—a small, glass tube about six inches long with a sort of bowl at the bottom where the meth had to be melted with a mini torch.

We were all high, all drinking. And then Jim woke up from a dead sleep, raging. This happens sometimes—often, actually—when people are coming down from a high. Their moods are messed up; they get mean; they get violent. Jim was probably mad that Cindy didn't wake him up when a bunch of free meth showed up in his apartment.

Whatever the reason for his fury, he was up in Cindy's face, screaming like a lunatic, cursing, and talking crazy. It was the dead of night in San Diego. Everything in the neighborhood was perfectly quiet, and since it doesn't get extremely hot, a lot of the neighbors had their windows open. Jim's screaming was harsh and ferocious and cruel. But worst of all, it was loud. When you're in an apartment with a couple lines of meth in your system and two more ounces in your jacket, loud is your enemy. Loud wakes the neighbors; loud gets the cops called.

We tried to calm Jim down before anyone woke up and called the police. But Jim wouldn't be calmed. The other two guys made a dash out the front door. I would have too, except that I was scared for Cindy. She was a tiny thing—blond, thin, and petite—maybe 5'2," while Jim was over six feet tall and muscular. He was pulling her hair, still screaming like a madman, and I was worried he was going to hit her; or worse.

Since his rage was only channeled at Cindy, I tried to talk him down. "Hey. You need to knock it off before the cops come. The neighbors are going to call. You don't wanna get caught with this crap in your house." I knew I sure didn't, but none of my rational reasoning did any good. Jim's voice was getting louder, eyes wild, face so close to hers, cuss words and deranged accusations breaking open the night.

At this point, so much time had passed that I was afraid to go out the front door, afraid the cops were on their way. I should point out that this wasn't necessarily true. You have to remember that I had been very high, and that a certain level of paranoia sometimes comes with the high or the come down afterwards. Still, I was convinced that the cops had been called and were on their way, knew it as though I heard sirens tearing through the streets.

I was the dealer. I had to leave, but at that point I couldn't risk being seen. So I decided to climb out the bathroom window. It seemed easy. It was just a story and a half up. I would hang my legs out and then scoot my butt down, drop a few feet and I was free. Jim was still screaming. I could hear him through every wall, every door.

I hung my legs out of the window, but then somehow lost my balance and tipped out too soon. My right leg got caught in a small tree that was just to the side of the window, and as I fell, my leg stayed caught, flipping me upside down. Now I dangled by the foot that was caught in the tree—my head about a foot and a half from the ground. A Bugs Bunny cartoon in action. If Bugs Bunny was ever out in the middle of the night trying to quietly sneak away from the cops because he was carrying two ounces of crystal meth in his pocket.

Even as I struggled upside down in the tree, I could hear Jim continue to scream.[1]

My foot that was caught in the tree was numb—a fact I didn't worry about, a fact I was even grateful for as I jerked my leg repeatedly, trying to release my foot from the branches of the tree. I was wearing brand new red suede cowgirl boots that went up about mid-calf. I loved those boots, and I was pretty ticked that I was getting them dirty. The boot that was caught up in the branch held my leg in a straight line. Eventually, I pulled the boot with my foot in it loose and my body came toppling down to the parking lot area behind the apartment buildings.

I stood up and heard a pop. Such a simple sound. *Pop.* The sound bubblegum makes on the inside of your mouth, the sound of a jar opening, a cork releasing.

After the pop, the pain was excruciating, sickening. I couldn't stand on my leg. I needed to get to a phone so I could call someone to pick me up. To do that, I needed to get to someone's apartment. I was still determined not to be seen by the cops, not to go to jail, but my plans for a simple getaway were over. I could not walk at all, so I would hop a time or two, then get down on my left side and do a crooked little army crawl, dragging my bad leg, still in the cowgirl boot, behind me until I couldn't bear it anymore. Then I would stand up again and hop once or twice, then back to the ground.

I did this through the length of that back parking lot and finally, after what felt like years, I got to the first apartment and knocked on the door. No one answered. That meant that I had to crawl-hop my way another apartment length to the next door. Mercifully, someone opened the door. And even more mercifully, I could lie my way through anything, even with a broken leg in the middle of the night. "I'm so sorry," I said, "but I was at my friend's house and her husband is flip-ping out and I couldn't stay. I hurt myself coming out, had an accident, need a ride. Can I use your phone?" Ironically, most of what I said was true.

A friend came to get me. He couldn't call an ambulance because I still had the meth on me, so I went to his house, stashed the meth, then called an ambulance.

By the time I got to the ER, I was in shock. My leg had a compound fracture—the tibia and fibula both broken and poking out through the skin on my leg. The pop I'd heard had been the bones breaking through my skin. The boot had held them in somewhat, acting as a sort of loose cast and keeping the bones from coming out further, which was good. Those boots had probably saved my leg. But the bones poking outside of my skin weren't my worst enemy. Inside my leg were the other halves of those broken bones—ragged and broken themselves. These inner bones, not held properly in place with all my hopping and scooting, had slid and bumped their way around in my leg, tearing through tissue and nerve, destroying much of it. When the ER sent me to surgery, the surgeon took one look at me and said, "What happened?"

"I slipped on my steps."

"No, you didn't."

"Yes, I did."

I didn't know that he and the ER doctor had probably seen dozens, maybe hundreds, like me—addicts, abused wives, suicidal teens, prostitutes. I didn't realize that some doctors, in addition to learning how to tend the sick of body, had to learn how to weave their way through the troubled minds of the sick in spirit, to discern the lies that fell like honey off our lips. I didn't realize we were such a common, predictable breed.

The surgeon did not smile at me, did not believe me. It is very safe to say he did not like me. But even so he looked at me and said, "I'm going to try like hell to save your leg, but I can't make any promises."

And he did save my leg—fitted with screws and pins like a cyborg princess.

---

1. Hanging upside down from that little tree, I could have premiered on America's Dumbest Criminals before the show even started.

CHAPTER TEN

I went back home and ignored most of the doctor's orders to stay off my leg. Sure, I rested for a bit, and I used crutches for months. But staying off my leg completely was not something I could do. I was busy. Each day as soon as I woke up, I was receiving calls on my pager from buyers, meeting them different places, doing business. I had three different pagers—one for my best customers, one for the others, and one for family. At the time I lived with two female roommates, who would watch my daughter for me when I had to run off. They knew what I was doing. Everybody knew what I was doing. They were doing it too. Every single person I knew was using drugs—one big happy family. As dealer, I was the matriarch.

Being a young, white, female drug dealer in the '90s was a lot like being a rock star. Everybody wanted to be my friend; anybody was happy to be my roommate; sure they'd watch my daughter. I had a whole crew of people willing to watch my daughter when she got home from school if I was gone.

I was so street smart—able to get and sell drugs, picking

up my supply in one of the worst parts of town, meeting addicts at various places. I was tough too—fracturing my leg in two places, then crawl-hopping through a parking lot, before straight-up lying to the face of the surgeon who saved me. And yet I was so naïve—willing to let my daughter stay with my druggie friends who were willing to watch her. [1]

Even when I was with my daughter, I was not really there —busy or high or buzzed or all three—my pager beeping, a call about where to meet the next customer. And then I was driving around, doing my business.

I gave Phoebe a lot of stuff, but I never made her healthy meals; I never provided her with discipline or routine. We were moving constantly to different apartments to live with different people (always women). I was often gone at night. I was often high in the morning when I got her off to school. Which isn't to say I didn't care. Which isn't to say I didn't have any standards for my child or our family life.

First: She always had food in her belly. I'm not saying it was nutritious food, but I never got so busy or high or wasted that I didn't provide food and clothing for my child. It was true that we had no schedule, no routine, no by-the-clock meals. But I was always sure to have cereal, milk, snacks and food at my house. If we were together, I'd take her out for a hamburger.

Second: I never took her with me or allowed buyers into my apartments. In fact, although she eventually knew that I used drugs, she never figured out that I sold them. When I asked her years later how it had hurt her to see me selling drugs, she had told me that at the time, she hadn't known what I was doing. I don't know if such a thing can be counted as a victory, but in my messed up, twisted life, I tried to shield her as much as I could, and I'm grateful she wasn't exposed to the selling part of my drug life.

Third: I never left her alone. Ever. She was always with a caregiver of some sort—a roommate or friend—all women, and all people I trusted.

So my friends watched my child while I sold. They watched her while I played. Sometimes to relax after a long day, I'd get dressed up—long green skirt with a slit up the leg, half shirt to show off my belly, black jacket over it with black fringe hanging off the edges, brushing my waist. Then I'd head to my favorite club. It was the place I went for plea- sure, not work. I'd do a line before I went (I had been up for eighteen to twenty hours by this time), then go and have a few drinks. I'd get home and fall into bed after three, and then be up at seven the next morning, ready to get back to work. Forget the cup of coffee; each morning I did a line to get moving.

And then one day in the winter of 1991 I was driving towards Ramona to fill an order for one of my clients when my roommate Jennie called. "The police are here; they're going to take Phoebe."

"What?" I felt the panic rise up. "What happened; why would they take her?"

She handed the phone to Officer Baxter—a man who's name I remember, though most of my roommates from the time have been forgotten. He was so nice, so calm, so sooth- ing. He told me I didn't come for Phoebe's follow up appoint- ments at the psychiatric facility, and that the police had to take her right now.

I begged him not to take her. I begged him to wait for me to get back. But he couldn't.

"I'm sorry, ma'am, but we have no choice: we have to take her."

I was hysterical—crying, screaming into the phone.

"But don't worry," he said, kind, soothing. "Just come

downtown and we'll get this sorted out in just a few minutes."

Maybe he just wanted me to shut up and calm down. Or maybe he meant it. Maybe he hoped I would be just as squeaky clean as I said I was, and that this was just a crazy goof-up after all. In fact, I'm sure he hoped that; I'm sure most cops do. But it wasn't. And it didn't take just a few minutes to get everything sorted out.

I had missed several of Phoebe's follow up appointments with the psychiatric facility. I had not even known that there were follow up appointments, although I can't say that that's because they didn't tell me. At the time, I had no sense of the future. I lived only in the now. I never made appointments for my drug dealing ahead of time. Everything operated on an "I'll be there in twenty minutes" basis. I'm pretty sure none of us—dealers or buyers—knew what twenty minutes meant. Twenty minutes was, "I'm coming now. I'll get there as soon as I can." Ten minutes, an hour and a half, whatever. It was all twenty minutes to us. The present. No past, no future. Twenty minutes was as far as we could see into the lives that lay ahead of us.

And Phoebe's follow up appointments had not been scheduled twenty minutes after she left. It had been a month, two months, I'm not even sure; and I'd missed them. Now they had my daughter at a place called Hillside—a home where kids could stay in temporary state custody. And, you may be asking, as I'm sure I did, how this could be done legally, how your child could be taken just like that?

I cannot even begin to tell you. Not because it is difficult or complicated (though it may be), but because I wasn't responsible and available enough at the time to process the things that were happening. Because of this, you and I are both going to have to piece the next few parts of this story together with a lot of *I'm assumings*.

I'm assuming that when I checked Phoebe out of the psychiatric facility I committed to come to a follow up appointment, perhaps even signed something. I'm assuming that a case worker was assigned to us. I'm assuming that the case worker contacted us, though I have no recollection of this ever happening. I'm also assuming that I was flagged. It must have been perfectly clear to any of the social workers and doctors I had contact with for the month that I came for my daily visits at the psychiatric facility that I was a drug addict.

To make matters worse, after Phoebe came home, she didn't always make it to school. Any time she told me she didn't feel well, which was often, I let her stay home. Additionally, people—my friends, remember them, those people who treated me like a rock star—had started to tattle on me. They didn't do it to be mean. They did it because in the drug world, as soon as you get caught by the cops, the first thing many people do is offer up somebody else's name—preferably somebody higher up on the food chain. In that way, you can get a lighter sentence or no sentence at all. That's what my "friends" did to me as soon as they were in a tight spot. Word about me must have started trickling into police reports and social workers' desks. Maybe there was no hard evidence, but it's not too much of a stretch to assume that people had their eyes on me.

It's just too bad that I didn't have my eyes on anything outside of myself. I might have been a little more prepared for some of the things that happened to me. As it was, any time something bad happened, it seemed to come at me with no warning, no logic—as though the fates simply had it in for me, trying to take away the things that mattered most.

In reality, I could have seen any number of tragedies coming if I'd bothered to look up for one second. In reality, there weren't monsters waiting at my door ready to tear down my life the first chance they got. In reality, there were just a bunch of normal, mostly kind people doing a hard and often heart-breaking job that revolved around people like me and the problems I created for myself and those I loved.

In my mind I had just missed a couple appointments—such a simple, normal oversight. Then these strangers had converged on my apartment in a seemingly non-sensical way —the caseworker and the cops, ready and able to take my child away from me when I wasn't there to protect her.

After that call from Officer Baxter, after they took my child, I went downtown immediately, which still took a good forty minutes. And I was told, "You can't see her right now. Everything is still being processed."

"But I need to pick up my daughter. She's not even supposed to be here."

"I'm sorry, we need to get this sorted out. You didn't show up for her follow up care."

I wanted to tell her what she could do with her follow up care, but for once I kept my mouth shut and waited until they finally let me see Phoebe. I ran to her and gave her a hug. She was seven years old. Seven years old and escorted from her house by a band of police officers when her mother wasn't there, then taken to Hillside for hours while the police "processed" who knows what.

I remember hugging my daughter and looking towards the open door. We could run for it. I could run with her out the door and get out of this place. We would find a new apartment, maybe cross the border. I had no idea—I couldn't think that far—again, only the now. And the now was screaming at me to run. For once I didn't listen to it. I stayed in that state custody house with my daughter and listened while a butt-lipped woman told me that Phoebe would have to stay overnight. In fact, she'd have to stay the whole weekend. "You'll have to go to court. Everything will be resolved there."

There was no room for argument. I would have to wait until Monday, when I would go to court and talk to a judge if I wanted to get Phoebe back. No amount of hysteria would change it. My daughter would be in temporary state custody for the weekend.

You can guess I dealt with it in the best possible way.

I STILL DIDN'T REALLY DOUBT THAT I WOULD GET MY daughter back. I would just calmly explain that I had missed her follow up appointments, and that it had just been a simple mistake. No big deal. Parents could miss a doctor's appointment here and there, right?

Apparently, not those appointments.

On Monday, when I showed up, I met a woman named Jan Ketchel. She was a tallish blond in her mid-forties. Thin with short, straight hair. Business. That's what Jan Ketchel was. She would be Phoebe's social worker. I hated her the minute I saw her. I knew that she was the wall standing between me and my child. And she was. They still wouldn't let me have my daughter back. She would be placed in a temporary foster situation and I would have to complete a parenting plan. This meant that I'd need to take parenting classes and be able to provide Phoebe with a stable home environment. Part of that meant getting our own apartment instead of hopping around from one friend's apartment to another. Also, I would have to take a drug test to show that I was clean.

Of course that was impossible. In order to get an apartment, I had to make money. In order to make money, I had to sell drugs. I had no other skills. I couldn't stand for any period of time on my leg, which meant I couldn't wait tables or even stand behind a counter. I figured I would just sell drugs until I got us an apartment and stashed away some savings. Then I would worry myself about the drug test. It made perfect sense to me.

Unfortunately, as you may guess, such a plan didn't make much sense to anyone who mattered. A couple weeks after my first court date, I went back to court, fully expecting to get my daughter back despite the fact that I hadn't done a single thing that they had told me I needed to do.

In the years that would come, I would always expect to get her back every time I went to court. I had no reason to expect this. I did not spend my time doing the things I was supposed to do. I did not get off drugs or get my own apartment[2] or prepare for the future. I *did* love my daughter. I *did* want her back. But I didn't understand at the time how to form that desire into the actions that would fulfill it. My life carried me and I rode with it. I never stopped it or took the steps necessary to control it. If you had asked me at the time, I would have told you that wasn't possible—that life handed you what it handed you, and you took it.

So I showed up at court. The judge sat in front of me and said that he'd received a letter. I'll always remember the next words he spoke. "It is a letter from your own mother."

My own mother? What did my own mother have to do with this? She lived in Florida. She knew nothing about my situation. Nothing about me. How she even knew to send a letter to a judge because I was appearing in court, I had no idea. But apparently, she believed me to be incapable of taking care of my child because in that letter she said,

"Don't give Phoebe back to my daughter; my daughter is on drugs."

I felt like all the air left the room.

Later I would learn that the court had contacted her as a potential guardian for Phoebe. She had refused. My own mother had refused her granddaughter. It was another wedge in the tree trunk that was our dying relationship. She would write a letter to a judge saying that I couldn't care for my child, while she—the grandmother—refused to do so.

I felt utterly betrayed.[3] I didn't care that what she'd written was true. I didn't care how my mom knew that I was on drugs. I didn't care about anything. After I left court—without Phoebe—I called my mom screaming, wild, enraged. That phone call was the last time I would talk to my mother for the next three and a half years.

I never wanted to see or speak with her again.

Much later—years later—I would learn why she had refused to take Phoebe. There had been practical reasons. Her health was declining and Phoebe was a fantastically strong and undisciplined child. But there was a bigger reason, a deeper reason, a reason that once I was sober I could finally understand. My mother knew that if she took my child, I would never recover—that I would always have a crutch, a person to care for my daughter and that because of that, I would never have the motivation to stop using drugs and pull myself together. My mother knew me a little better than I thought she knew me. She knew I loved Phoebe. She knew I loved her even more than I loved drugs. She knew that if no one stepped up to take that child, I would eventually pull myself together enough to get my baby back. My mother bet everything on that horse.

Later, much later, she would tell me she was sorry for sending that letter and I would tell her I was glad she did. But

I couldn't see later. And in the moment—at a time in life when I only knew the moment—there was no one I thought I hated more than my mother.

There was someone, however, who came close. Jan Ketchel. Since showing up at that first court date, she'd managed to make herself an unpleasant fixture in my life. Or rather she'd managed to make herself a fixture in Phoebe's life, which I found unpleasant for my own life.

Jan Ketchel never saw anything good in what I was doing. She didn't see the visits I made to the foster home or the presents I brought. Nope. At every court appearance she always said the same thing. "The mother doesn't yet have a stable residence. The mother hasn't fulfilled the parenting plan."

I mean, it wasn't like I wasn't trying. I'd gone to at least two of the required parenting classes. And I was trying to get settled. There were just things I needed to do first. First. Jan Ketchel didn't understand *first*. If I could just get her to move, to budge, then maybe I could make some progress. But Jan Ketchel did not budge. I would have Phoebe back when I had an apartment, a legal income, and a series of clean drug tests. No sooner.

Originally, Phoebe was sent to a family who had several foster children. Several months in, the father of that family hit one of the foster children. After that, they were all reassigned.

In my mind, this would have been the perfect time to get Phoebe back. I mean, were they really going to ship my daughter out to a new home every few months? Surely, putting her with me would be a better idea. But Jan Ketchel didn't agree. Phoebe was sent to a woman named Sabra Bradley.

Sabra was a tall, black woman with more grace in her pinky than I had in my whole body. Technically, Sabra just had a small family—she and her son. But she also had a fiancée who didn't live with her and a bunch of other foster kids, who did live with her. Sabra loved those kids. Several months after she took Phoebe in, she moved out to the country so that she could raise the kids in a safer neighborhood, so that she could get a bigger house with a couple of horse stables, so that they could have animals and room to move. Sabra bought two horses—Dandelion and Brown Sugar—whose colors matched their names. Additionally, hordes of kittens and other little wild creatures roamed the land for the kids to play with and experience.

Phoebe had a beautiful room. Sabra had made the curtains and a valance to match the bedspread—a white background with a green leaf pattern. She was a talented seamstress and she sewed it all herself. For the valances, she'd taken a sheet that matched the bedspread, doubled it over, and stuffed it so that it had a poufy ballooned look. Perfect for a young girl in the '90s. Throughout the house, much of the other furniture was white and gold.

I don't know how she did it with all those kids running around. Sabra had excellent taste, was a fantastic householder and cook, and most of all, she had a lot of love in her heart.

Her house in the country was about twenty minutes from my bummed rental in the not-city. Which was great. But, since I didn't have a valid driver's license, I had to mooch rides for my visits with Phoebe.

I should point out that not having a license wasn't the thing that kept me from driving. Normally, I drove around wherever I pleased, not worrying about whether it was legal or not. What kept me from driving to visit Phoebe was my lawyer. He told me, "Don't bother to show up if you're driving yourself in a car. The foster parent has to keep track of these things, and she'll know you're driving illegally;

she'll report you." So I bummed rides from friends. Several times, I showed up on the back of a motorcycle with my buddy Gary even though motorcycles terrified me. The truth was that I would do just about whatever I had to in order to see my daughter.

I always had a welcome spot at Sabra's house. And her table. Once, when I showed up around dinner time, she invited me to eat with the family. The food was amazing, home-cooked and delicious. I literally never cooked anything from scratch for myself. When I ate—which I didn't always do as a meth addict—it was out of a box, can, or drive through. I wasn't used to eating homemade food, much less homemade food prepared with so much skill. At the end of the meal, Sabra told me I could come over and have dinner with them any time.

Often, after dinner, as I helped Sabra clean up, she would look at me and say, "How long since you've gotten high?"

"Two weeks," I would say every time. *Two weeks*. It was a lie. It was always a lie. Two weeks was what we all said when we were trying to recover. Telling Sabra it had been two weeks was like a drunk guy telling the cop who pulled him over he had only had two beers. Two weeks was not perfect, but acceptable. A progressive length of time. An effort that said you were getting closer, gaining control, making progress. But it was never two weeks. And I know Sabra knew it.

SPEAKING OF TIME, I REALIZED I'D HAD MY CAST ON MY LEG for what seemed like a long time. I was getting sick of it and wanted to get it taken off. No problem. I would just call the doctor's office and schedule an appointment to get it taken off. Except…guess what? Apparently, the doctor's office had already scheduled a follow up appointment, but I'd missed it. Don't worry. No big deal, right? I mean, people miss appointments sometimes. (Wait, does this sound familiar?)

It must have sounded a little too familiar to the receptionist too, because when I asked her when I could schedule a new appointment, she said, "You missed your follow up appointment. The doctor won't see you." Not a beat of time to think about it, not a pause to consider my leg.

"Seriously?" I asked. "What am I supposed to do?"

"Go to Urgent Care," the receptionist told me, and then she hung up the phone.

At Urgent Care, they did see me. They cut a line down the front of my cast so they could take it off. Except that when they opened it up, they saw the results of my lack of follow up care. I had twelve three-inch staples near my ankle on the top part of my foot. They had grown black mold. The good people of the Urgent Care wouldn't touch it with a ten-foot pole. "You need to go back to the person who put this on. We can't take it off." They taped up my cast—as in they literally taped up the part that they had cut open—and sent me on my way.

I called my original doctor again. He would not see me. He had saved my leg in the first place—done an intensive surgery on a woman with no insurance, a woman he knew had lied to his face about the injury. And he'd scheduled a follow up appointment. I'd missed it. And I guess his charity or patience or both had run out. Often doctors are only allowed to do so much charity work per year. Why waste it on the doper who's going to miss her appointment while weakening her bones through her drug habit?

I went home, cut through the tape the Urgent Care had put on my cast, and took it off myself. Then I soaked my leg in Epson salts every night. In the space between my staples, I could see a thick white tendon. I hoped it wouldn't get infected. It didn't, and the mold went away. Eventually, I started picking the staples out. There. Good as new. Who needs a trauma surgeon for follow up care anyway? Or physical therapy? Or a healthy lifestyle? Not me. I was just fine.

---

1. When I look back, I'm grateful that all of those people I left Phoebe with did take care of her, at least well enough. None of them abused or neglected her.

2. I couldn't get my own apartment because I could never provide pay stubs or prove I had an income.

3. Most of the time when a judge gets a letter from a family member, it says something like, "I know my son's a drug addict, but he's really a good person." Or, "I know my child robbed a bank, but she has a sweet heart; please be lenient on her." Even Jeffrey Dahmer's dad would visit him in prison.

CHAPTER ELEVEN

In addition to being a leg-nurse-in-training, it turns out that I was a fantastic business woman. My drug "business" grew, and it grew quickly. Most drug dealers would get a big chunk of drug and then they could divide it into smaller portions that were more expensive (like buying milk by the gallon versus milk by the quart). But most dealers wouldn't just divide it. Most would "cut it." When they cut it, they'd add impurities to it—usually another powder like a baby laxative or vitamin B12. They would add this to the meth and then "re-rock it"—cook it again so it was crystalized, though it now had a cutting agent in it, making it less potent.

I didn't cut my meth. I only sold the pure drug and I sold it in larger amounts. Because of this, people would come to me when they wanted the "good stuff." Word got around—to other users, and to other dealers as well. I helped that along.

Many users had several dealers they would buy from (just like you probably have several grocery stores where you're willing to shop). In that way, if one dealer didn't have any drug or you couldn't get a hold of them or they'd been thrown in jail, you still had a source you could go to get your drugs. Soon, I started telling my customers to tell their other suppliers to get their drugs from me because mine was the best. In fact, I gave my users a one-gram "sample" to take to their supplier (this pure sample was worth about eighty dollars in the '90s.)

Then, if their suppliers started coming to me to buy their drug, I would give my customers a free eight ball (3.5 grams —worth about one hundred fifty to three hundred dollars depending on how you broke it down and/or cut it if you sold it). For every additional ounce their other suppliers bought from me, they got another free eight ball. With this reward system, I kept my buyers as honest as I could keep a group of drug addicts. My buyers preferred the continual freebies to the one stolen chunk, and they knew I had the best drug, so they didn't want to get cut off by stealing from me.

As for me, it meant that instead of selling a measly two hundred dollar portion to my buyers, I started selling much larger sixteen hundred dollar portions to their suppliers. Clearly, I could have rocked it with Mary Kay.[1]

Soon enough all my customers' suppliers were coming to me for the good drugs, then cutting them and selling them for their own profits.

I liked the arrangement. It was less risky than cutting the drug and selling little portions to tons of people. What I didn't fully realize was that through the arrangement I'd moved up yet again. From dealer to supplier. What I did realize was that I was making a crap load of money.[2] And I liked that I felt I could still maintain a sort of standard. My drugs were clean. No one was being given the short-shrift.

In this way I made a lot of contacts and even a few friends.

Matt was my partner. When I say he was my partner, I mean that he bought from me and we became close. He was my favorite addict/seller of all time. He was a skinny tall guy who was a welder by day and then sold drugs on the side. He was married to a woman named Trisha who was a serious addict—obese with diabetes and no teeth. Trisha had a best friend named Lilly, who lived with them and also used. I loved them to pieces. I would sell to Matt and he would cut the crap out of his drugs, and sell to his own people.

Matt was one of the only true friends I had when I was in the drug business. Some nights when we were bored and high, he would call William Tong—the demon who molested my daughter and never got caught. The phone would ring, Tong would pick up, and Matt would say in an extremely creepy voice, "I know what you did to those little girls. I'm looking into your window. I can see you. And I'm going to kill you." Then he'd hang up and we'd laugh like high hyenas. It was the only revenge I ever got on that evil man. It wasn't enough, but it was something.

Tong was scared. "You can't harass me like this," he'd say. Want to bet? We could. And we did.[3]

Matt and I were partners for about a year. Until he got arrested. Matt was coming home after a very long shift. He was tired. He was probably falling asleep a little, weaving over the line. He wasn't even high. Just exhausted. A cop pulled him over and it would have been a simple warning, an exchange between two tired working-class men. Except that Matt was so tired he'd left a half-ounce bag of meth sitting on the seat in his truck.

While Matt was in jail, I kept Trisha and Lilly supplied with drugs. I also brought them bags of groceries, checking in on them regularly to make sure that they were okay. Since Trisha had diabetes, I would buy loads of Healthy Choice dinners and fill up her freezer with them. I didn't cook at all, didn't even know how, and I wasn't willing or able to come into their house and clean it, but I tried to care for them in any way that I could, especially in the ways it seemed they were incapable of caring for themselves.

Because of Matt's arrest, and others just like it, I was meticulous about not being pulled over. I was always driving without a license. This meant that every time I got in my car, I checked the taillights, headlights, and blinkers. I'd known so many dealers get pulled over for a simple infraction. One taillight out, and you were busted. I wasn't going to let that happen to me.

For a while things were not half bad; for a while I felt safe. I had my business. I had faithful customers. I had my methods. I protected myself and my friends by never selling from my house or apartment, and I lived with a level of comfort. I could have lived with a higher level of comfort if my life hadn't been so risky.

At the time, I lived in a 5,500 square foot house with a friend and two other roommates. The house was at the top of a long drive with a steep hill. The floors were all wood, the living room had a beautiful fireplace, the kitchen was open just as that concept was coming into style. There was a loft, a pool table, a swimming pool, and sauna. I never got to enjoy that house. All I did was stop by to pick up some clothes and take a shower. Then I would go stay in hotels, which is where I did my business. But just as I didn't cut my drugs and give people a crap product, I didn't sell drugs out of a cock-roach-crawling Motel 6.

In San Diego, there were a bunch of hotels for tourists. This area was called "Hotel Circle" and there must have been at least a hundred hotels in this area. It was easy to find coupons for them in maps or entertainment books that were all over town. I'd get myself a coupon for $39/night on a hotel that normally cost $109/night. Then I'd call the hotel and make a reservation using my real first name and a fake last name.

About an hour before I was supposed to check in, I'd call the hotel frantically. "Oh my gosh; I've just lost my wallet. I don't have my cards or my driver's license. I don't know what to do. I'm not sure how I'm even going to check in."

"Oh, don't worry about it," they'd tell me every single time. "It'll be fine. When you get here, we'll get you taken care of."

Then I would show up at the hotel, pay cash, and no one ever knew who I was or had a way to track me. It would never work now with computer systems and check-ins, but back then it worked like a charm. And with so many hotels in the area to go to, I never got caught.

To treat myself, I started getting the honeymoon suites, soaking in the hot tubs, enjoying as much as I could all the money I was making. Because in a lot of ways, I couldn't enjoy my money at all. I'd always loved clothes, cars, possessions. I'd always wanted a bunch of money to buy a bunch of things.

Now I had the money, but as my drug business grew, a friend pulled me aside and told me, "You've got to dress down, keep a low profile." Away went the Italian leather shoes and black fringe jackets. Now I wore jeans and a t-shirt. I drove a plain car when I drove a car at all.[4] It was important as a dealer to hide what you had so you didn't get caught, robbed, or hurt. Thus, ironically, I had plenty of money, but I stopped going to clubs, stopped wearing the clothes I liked, couldn't get a smoking hot car, and had to avoid the big beautiful house I was renting.

I was still young, still pretty. But all that did was make people suspicious of me. Everybody thought I was a fed. It was hard to earn their trust. In fact, I've never worked so hard in my life as I did at that time in my life. I was always busy, always working to make and keep my contacts, to stay out of the sight of the cops while staying in sight for my clients.

Those hotel hot tubs were all I had.[5]

BEYOND NOT HAVING THE STUFF I'D ALWAYS WANTED, MY life was also a little lacking in the people department. I had my clients, and a few people who called themselves friends— some were; some weren't. But I had no daughter, no real boyfriends, and not much contact with my family. I still wasn't speaking to my mother. And I only talked to my father infrequently—sometimes as little as every eight months. When you're on drugs, you have no concept of time or how much time has passed. I would call my dad every so often in tears over what Mom had done or to vent about something else—basically when I was really down. I would give him a number to call me and then it would be lost or changed or my pager would get stolen, so that when he tried to contact me, he couldn't. This left all the contact up to me, and I wasn't exactly good at it.

My dad didn't say anything, didn't criticize; he just wanted to be there. Later I would learn that he used to stay awake at night, worrying about whether I was alive. Still, every few months when I called, he sat patiently and listened. He was the only one I had any kind of communication with through most of that time in my life.

My oldest brother struggled with a mental illness and my brother, Randy, was busy with his own young family. Which was fine with me. I was constantly mad at Randy. He had always been a goody two shoes tattletale who didn't support me or my lifestyle anyway. To deepen the divide, he'd joined the Mormon Church[6], which took his lifestyle even further away from mine. We couldn't be more different. But my little brother, Robert, the one I was closest to—was living in San Francisco.

Me with three protective (and better behaved) brothers

I didn't know this. If I had maybe we could have gotten together. As it was, only he knew we were sharing a state, and I wasn't making it easy for him to find me. Years later, I would learn that he had paged me numerous times, but I'd never recognized the number, so I'd never called him back.

Robert didn't have much more than my number. He knew I was living in San Diego, but he didn't have an accurate address. The truth is that I barely knew where I was living myself—shifting around like I did from hotel to hotel, stopping into the house I rented only to grab some clothes or take a shower. Even if Robert had found out where I lived and had come asking around for me, someone would have sent him away. After all, I was spending a significant amount of effort trying *not* to be found. Of course, I hadn't meant to include my little brother in that. I would have loved to have seen him. But since I didn't know he was living just a few hours north of me, and he didn't know where to find me, we never got the chance to hang out together.

Not that Robert didn't try. One weekend Robert came down to San Diego looking for me. He had nothing but some old apartment numbers, maybe a few outdated contacts.

I didn't know—wouldn't know till years after his death—that my closest brother had spent a weekend searching through San Diego for his older sister. And never finding her. He looked up old addresses, asked around, called people. I was nowhere. And so, at the end of the weekend, he went back home to San Francisco—to his life with friends who could be found and people who would return his calls.

It was the last time I would have had the chance to see him—alive or dead. Two years later, he was flying in a small plane with his buddies when it went down over the San Francisco Bay. They searched for days for the bodies, but only found one. It wasn't my brother. My little brother was gone, never to be recovered. Just like the days he'd spent looking for a sister who wouldn't be found. Just like the years of my life that slipped like sand through my fingers.

My brother, Randy, didn't tell me that Robert had come looking for me until I had been sober for years. He knew I would be crushed when I heard it. He was right.

---

1. Just think: If my life had gone a different direction when I was in my 20's, I'd be driving a pink Cadillac now instead of limping around on a gimpy leg.
2. I was making about 20K/month. But I spent a lot on clothes and beauty

products. Plus, my overhead was pretty high. I was practically living out of hotel rooms in order to hide from the police. If I fronted someone and they got caught, I would lose the money they owed me. Plus, I would bail them out of jail so they didn't rat me out.

3. Remember, we were using land lines. There was no caller ID, no *69. There was no way for him to track us.

4. Since I didn't have a valid driver's license, I couldn't buy a car, but I had some friends that had a used car dealership. They would loan me a car, which I'd drive for a few months, and then they'd loan me another one.

5. That, and an occasional trip to Nordstroms to buy my favorite perfumes, bubble baths, and face creams. The cops couldn't see skin care on me. It was an invisible indulgence.

6. The real name is The Church of Jesus Christ of Latter-day Saints, but the only thing I'd ever heard was "Mormon."

CHAPTER TWELVE

About two years after I'd been dealing I took some groceries to Trisha and Lilly and noticed a man in front of their apartment. Though I couldn't remember making the appointment that would have kept my daughter out of foster care, I remember that man with perfect clarity. I saw him through the window. He stopped, looked at the apartment, and then walked all the way around the building. That night I was supposed to go pick up some drugs. For some reason I was getting a ride. I can't remember if I didn't have a car at the time or if I just wanted to use a different car. We did that, switching out vehicles so we wouldn't be as easy to catch. My ride showed up, but with him was some guy I didn't know. I didn't like that. On our way to San Diego, this guy I didn't know kept naming landmarks on the way, "Oh look, there's the Grossmont Hospital; they've re-done the front entrance." "Man, I used to go to that McDonald's on 4th street." Something was off. Because, you see, in addition to my business savvy and acting skills, I also had a pretty decent sixth sense.

I was supposed to pick up my drugs at someone's house,

but instead I told them to stop at Jack in the Box. I went in, ordered a soda, and chatted with a couple of guys. It looked like I'd met my connection.

At the Grossmont and La Mesa exit, twelve cop cars showed up. They pulled us over and had everyone get out like a felony stop. "Driver, out with your hands up. Passenger, out of the car. Middle passenger, come out with your hands up." They were all there with their flashlights. All three of us had to lie on the gravel with our faces on the ground. "Laura Findlay," they asked. Yup, that was me. It was scary at first—that they had me flat on the ground, that they knew my name. My name. Someone had given it to them. Maybe more than one someone. But I didn't have any drugs on me, which meant they didn't have anything on me. And I knew it.

I went from scared to mouthy pretty quick. They took us into the station because there was a gun in the car, though no drugs. Within minutes, I was talking smack. "Oh my gosh. You guys are so smart. You caught me transporting oxygen."

It wasn't the best choice of my life (what was?). There's nobody a cop likes to bust better than a fancy drug dealer who runs her mouth.

———

A FEW MONTHS LATER, I DID GET BUSTED. ALL TOLD I'M NOT entirely sure how many times I went to jail. I'm going to say it was about thirteen times in three years. Most of the time, I didn't stay long. Most of the time, I didn't have to go past the holding cell. Not that the holding cell was exactly Disneyland.

The first time I landed myself in the holding cell, it was surreal. I still felt, after all, that I was a normal person. I remember thinking, "How could I be *here*, like a regular criminal?" I wasn't a thief or rapist or extortionist. As far as I was concerned, I was just a step up from tending bars.

The holding cell, for anyone who may not have spent her twenties and thirties getting arrested, is a small cell where they keep you for a day or two while they try to figure out what they're going to do with you. It's from there that you can be bailed out. It's from there they can decide whether you're going to go to jail or not. There are usually six to seven women in the holding cell and they would keep us there anywhere from an hour to two days.

Inside the holding cell, it was cold. I suppose they wanted to keep the stink down. People in the holding cell were all of different races and nationalities—a veritable melting pot. It smelled like one, too. We might have all looked different, but after being in the holding cell for a couple of days, we all smelled the same. There were several wooden benches for sitting or sleeping, concrete floors, no blankets or furniture. You weren't allowed to bring jackets in, which meant you couldn't so much as roll anything up to use as a pillow. When the police shut the big blue door that locked us in, all we had left to look through was one long, narrow window—a portal through which we could see a small part of the police station, a tiny part of the world.

If you've ever watched a cop show, you know the window, but you don't know the filth because they don't show it. They should because it's always there. Fingerprints and streak marks from bodily fluids, oils, sweat, spit, snot. Some streaks were thick like finger paint, others smudgy or milky.

Fingerprints weren't all you got to enjoy in the holding cell. Sometimes prostitutes would come in with sores up and down their arms from shooting heroine or meth or both, their faces scratched and scabbed from compulsive picking. The sores were open wounds, often infected with green and yellow puss. These women would go into the infirmary to have their abscesses lanced.

While they were doing that, other women would lie on the floor, holding their stomachs, having diarrhea and vomiting at the same time. The more seasoned criminals would ask, "Are you kickin?'" I didn't know what that meant my first few times. I would learn later that it meant they were in withdrawal from heroine. Some of the women would sit by them, try to comfort them while another woman from the main jail who was on cleaning duty came in with a stringy mop and bleach to clean up the waste. It still turns my stomach to think of that smell. It was the smell of crime.

If you walked into the cell and moved off to the left, you'd find a bathroom. It wasn't hard to find because all that concealed it was half of a concrete wall. In this way, when you went to use the lidless steel bowl of a toilet, anyone who wanted or needed to could see your top half sitting there on the commode, though your bottom half was concealed. You know what wasn't concealed? Any scents that happened to arise from you doing your business. Women could stay in the holding cell for up to forty-eight hours. Inevitably somebody had to poop; inevitably somebody was on her period. If people wanted, they could watch you grunt or listen to the crinkle of a sanitary napkin[1].

When you came out, there was a small steel sink with cheap soap and thin, brown paper towels. There was also a phone. Yes, inside our cozy cell, and for reasons I don't quite understand, the holding cell telephone was located close to the concrete and steel bathroom.

The phone looked like a pay phone, only it was free. When you dialed a number from it, it would give your loved one this message. "This is a free call from the California

Corrections." There's nothing to warm a mother's heart like that. The phone was just as dirty as the window and worse— grimy, caked on dirt, oils, smear marks—decades of gross packed into each little crevice of the phone. And, as opposed to the window, which you just looked through, you got to hold the phone up to your face.

I hated that phone, always tried to keep it away from my skin. But I would still use it. We all would. Every time, every chance we had. I never saw a fight break out over the phone[2], but it was a precious commodity. If you spent too much time on it, the other women in the holding cell would get restless, "Hey, you've had enough time. Get off the phone."

Some of the women made their calls hard faced, heavy voiced. Others stuttered and cried. Watching people make their calls, it was easy to see that the women in the holding cell were a strange mix of hard criminals and greenies who'd never been in jail before.

I was at a weird place in between—hardly a dangerous criminal, but hardly a newbie either. After a while, I learned to use my time pretty well while in the holding cell. By which I do not mean that I got to work writing the next great American novel.

WHEN YOU'RE IN THE HOLDING CELL, YOU USUALLY HAVE A bail. That means that someone can "bail you out." We all know what that means. Or at least we all think we do. Some bails are set low—at, say, one thousand dollars. Some are set high at, say, fifty thousand dollars. If the bail is low, a friend or relative can often come pay to bail you out, but when it's set high, no one can. When that happens, someone will some- times agree to come sign for you. This means that they— acting as a responsible citizen—sign you out, and agree to get you to court for your court date, often offering up the deed for their house or other collateral.

If you show up for court, you don't have to pay your bail and neither do they. If you don't show up for court, then things get more complicated.

And many of us don't show up for court. Even if we had wanted to (which we don't), we were users and dealers and criminals. We didn't keep track of things like court dates set a month in advance. But like I said, we don't want to show up anyway. So we don't. Which isn't great for the person who bailed us out.

While it's true that the system doesn't come in and take their house or car or ten thousand dollars right away, I suppose they could. Usually, though, they send out bounty hunters first. That's right—bounty hunters—like on Star Wars. These bounty hunters look for you—the criminal who didn't show up for court. If your mom or boyfriend signed to bail you out, they might not have to pay right away, but the bounty hunters will come to their house every day, they'll ask where you are, they'll try to get phone numbers. And usually that mother or boyfriend will eventually give them information, especially if they don't want to get stuck giving up their house or retirement savings to pay for your loser butt. In this way, the bounty hunters find you, and the process begins again. Each time you get arrested for the same level crime, your bail gets higher. Naturally, it eventually gets a little harder to get someone to come and bail you out.

If you don't appear and a cop pulls you over because your head light is out, or your blinker didn't work, or you exceeded the speed limit, he pulls up your information and an FTA (Failure to Appear) warrant shows up. You wind up back in jail. Life gets harder. Enter the bail bondsman.

A bail bondsman is a person who will come to jail and

sign for you. Naturally he does this out of the goodness of his heart and wishes you the very best with your life and future. Oh wait. Nope. Naturally he does this because you, or someone you love, is going to pay him. You are going to pay him one tenth of what your bail would have been. So if your bail is set at ten thousand dollars, the bail bondsman gets one thousand dollars. He gets it whether you go to court or not, whether you run or not, whether the bounty hunters come after you or not. And, yes, there are a few catches. Because he wants his money and he knows that you, dear, are a criminal. So he'll sign you out of jail if someone will sign for you. A loved one will sign with him because they can't afford to pay your bail with the court, but they can leave some type of collateral with the bondsman and hope that you show up for court. If the bail is small, he'll just need a few paystubs. Otherwise, he'll need a title to your car, or you'd better have some decent equity in your house.

Then if you don't show up in court, he'll just send his own friendly neighborhood bounty hunters after you. They'll tell your mother or boyfriend loving things like, "You need to get in touch with your son/girlfriend. I wouldn't want you to lose your house. You'd better get in touch." Eventually the people with their butts on the line will convince you to show up in court, or they'll give those bounty hunters any information they need to find you. And then, eventually, you'll show up in court and he'll get to keep his money.

I got to be on pretty good terms with my bail bondsman. In fact, I started referring him to the other girls in my cell. There were always plenty of girls in need of some help—many in for the first time, scared and embarrassed. I'd say to them, "Do you need a bail bondsman? My bail bondsman will totally take care of you." As if we were talking about a real estate deal, not jail. In fact, when I would call my bail bondsman to get me out, he'd say, "I'll get you out for free, just get me some other people." Maybe I wasn't exactly great at showing up for court, but that didn't bother my bail bondsman too much because he knew I knew all the criminals, so he was happy to let me stay on with him. When I sent enough people his way, he would pay off my bail.

Multi-level marketing at its finest. And, I should be clear, that while being a bail bondsman is legal, offering kickbacks to your "clients" for finding you other clients, is not. After all, it's still not Mary Kay.

---

1. We got the huge Kotex pads that were thick and uncomfortable. They were so bulky, it felt like you had a pair of sweatpants rolled up in your underwear.
2. I DID see fights break out over the phone later when I was in jail.

CHAPTER THIRTEEN

No one ever comes up to you at fancy parties and says, "You know, you just meet the *best* people in jail." There's a reason for that (many probably), but the biggest reason is that you *don't* meet the best people in jail. Shocking, right? Unfortunately for me, I still hadn't figured it out.

One of the times I got out on bail and then proceeded to ignore my court dates, I met a girl at a party one night. I knew her. From jail. I remembered her because we shared a first name.

It was pretty obvious that she was down on her luck (as though she'd been up on her luck when we were in jail together). She was a skinny white biker chick with long hair. She looked rough, not at all like some of the high-functioning nurse/lawyer/accountant types that also bought drugs from me on occasion. Nope, this girl was the type that looked like a doper.

We shared some drinks and then, in a misplaced bout of compassion, I gave her an eight ball to help her get back on her feet. She could use a little, then break it up and sell the rest. It seemed like the right thing to do. In fact, in my drug dealing, I actually always felt like I was doing people a service (as if I was selling well-built tennis shoes, not mind- and life-altering substances). I always figured that these people were going to do drugs anyway, so I could give them what they wanted and needed. And I could give them the high quality stuff. Some people donate toys for tots or pay the toll for the guy behind them. I gave drugs to the wrong people.

A month or so after this, I had run out of stock and was heading to San Diego to re-up—to get more drugs from my supplier. I liked to get more before the first of the month, which is busy season, so to speak, in the drug world.[1] There's even a rap song about drugs called "The First of the Month."

I was getting a ride from a friend of a friend. And this friend of a friend first needed to go to somebody's house to pick up some money that was owed to him. Now, maybe if you've never been part of the drug culture, you can see that this sounds suspicious or unsafe. After all, I was driving around southern California with this guy I barely knew, and —since I'd been caught with a gun in the car once before—I was unarmed. Not only that, but this guy went into a house of people I'd never met, with the supposed intention to get money from them. And then, instead of it taking five minutes like it should have, I sat in the car and waited for a good twenty minutes.

If this had happened in a movie you were watching, you would have thought to yourself, "Hmm, something just isn't right about this." And if you saw me get out of the car to approach the house, you might have thought, "No, Laura, don't go in the house. Something is off about this situation." But I didn't get any of those warning cues. The thing was, none of it was that unusual in the drug world. We often went places with people we didn't know well, and they often needed to get money from other people. And it was hardly uncommon for users to lose track of time—for that five minute task to drag on for an hour. In the drug world, nobody ever knows what time it is or how much time has passed. By drug world standards there was no reason for me to be suspicious of this friend of a friend who had left me in the car to go into a stranger's house in an unfamiliar part of town and stay there way too long.

Besides, I always felt invincible as a dealer. The police were my only enemies. Everybody else was my best friend. Right? Which didn't mean that this guy's extended leave wasn't irritating. Because I had to pee.

When my bladder just couldn't handle it anymore, I got out of the car, and knocked on the door.

They let me in, just like that, then kicked the door shut. I was dragged into the bedroom by a bunch of biker thugs—nine of them—men and women. The friend of a friend who'd given me a ride and Biker Laura (whom I'd met at the bar a month earlier) knew each other. They had set me up. Since it seemed I was rich and powerful enough to just give away an eight ball, they figured I was dripping drugs. And they wanted some. They needed some. Didn't we all?

"Where's the dope?" They asked me over and over.[2]

"I don't have any," I told them. "I was just going to re-up."

The women dragged me into the bathroom, still asking me, "Where's the dope" and hitting me in the face every time I said I didn't have any.

Biker Laura leaned in and said, "I know she has dope on her." And then to me, "Tell us where it is now or we'll rip your guts out like a dead fish." And then to them, "She probably has it keistered."

You may know, even if you are not part of the drug community, what a keister is.[3] And if you do know, then you

117

might be able to take a guess at what it means when a drug is 'keistered.' When a drug is keistered, it's hidden, either in your anus or your vagina.

So when they were threatening to rip my guts out to find the drug, they weren't just talking tough. If necessary, they had every intention of ripping into whatever place they needed to in order to find the drugs they thought were hidden. In fact, they'd brought a huge machete into the bathroom with us.[4]

One of the girls searched me, inside and out. It was humiliating, but more than that, I was terrified that they were going to cut me up, from vagina to abdomen, looking for drugs. They didn't.

"There's nothing up here," the girl said. "She doesn't have any."

Biker Laura still insisted that I did, but the other woman was adamant. "There's nothing there."

Biker Laura held my hair. "You better call your connection and get him over here right now."

I wasn't going to call my connection. If I did, they'd have us both. I lied and told them that if they took me to a certain apartment, I could get some there. I don't remember what my great plan was—how I had hoped to escape when they took me to that other apartment. What I do remember is that as soon as they rushed me to their car, Biker Laura shoved a coat over my head and told me to stay low. She said, "If you move or try to get out of here, we're going to kill you." The other girl sat next to me with her elbow on me to hold me down.

It was then that I knew that they had done this type of thing before, and they would kill me if they had to. They didn't want to be seen with me, so if they killed me no one would know I'd been there. I knew then that I couldn't give them any drugs. If I did, I would become their property—to use and abuse whenever they needed or wanted something. I would have to talk my way out, or I would be killed.

When we got to the apartment, no one was there[5]. They shoved me back in the car and took me back to their place.

"Call your connection and get it," they told me.

"Look," I said. "If I call from here, he won't even know the number.[6] He won't call back. Listen, if you guys let me go, I'll get the dope for you. I'll go to my buddy's house and call my connection. He'll answer if I page him with that number. Just let me go."

One and a half days. That's how long they held me against my will in that horrible apartment. My face swelled up from the beating, one eye sealed shut, I ached from being searched and prodded. I didn't sleep. I was either in a chair or standing the entire time. Somebody was always watching me, even when I had to go to the bathroom.

One and a half days they argued, increasingly desperate, over what they should do to get their dope, how they should use me. As the hours stretched on, something had to be done. Some of them had to leave—they had families elsewhere, things they had to do. And the apartment wasn't theirs. They were borrowing it from another user—a *square user* as we called them. A square meant someone who had a job and was high functioning, but still an addict. This person must have agreed to let them use his apartment in exchange for some drugs, but soon he would need his house back.

"Listen," I told them. "It's only dope. I'll give it to you. It's no big deal. Just let me go and I'll get it."

There was no other choice. They wanted something that they knew I could get if I wanted to. "Let me go," I told them. "I'll call them from my friends' house. Then my supplier will recognize my number. You can get your drugs immediately."

Immediately. A word too sweet for them to ignore. "If you screw us over in any way, we'll kill you." They wanted a half pound of meth.

That was worth about forty-five hundred dollars to me. I would never even give them a line of drugs. I told them where to drop me off. It was at the end of Trisha and Lilly's street. It was a busy area with an apartment complex that had a laundry next door. People were coming and going. I knew no one from the biker group would follow me out because they didn't want to be seen with me—it would be a liability if they came after me later. They didn't want any visible connection to me at all. But they couldn't very well bag me up and carry me to someone's apartment in the middle of the day either. So they agreed to drop me off. And I agreed to get the meth and call them. I was a pretty good sweet talker; and, of course, a fantastic liar. And this was their only chance to get some drugs. They were willing to take it. They wanted to get high, but they also wanted the earning potential that a half pound of meth would give them. They could divide it up into much smaller portions and make thousands of dollars in profit.

They dropped me off and I turned my back on them with a parting obscenity. I waited in the crowded area until they drove off and then I went to Trisha and Lilly's. My face was swollen, purple. My hair was a mess. My clothes were wrinkled. The women fawned over me. "Laura, what happened?"

As soon as they knew, we called some friends. They came over with guns and bats. "Let them try and get you," they said. "No one's going to touch you." "I've got something for them if they come."

But I was still afraid. I could talk tough and walk tough. But I knew that they still might come back for me. And I was terrified.

That night I went to get a shower. I hadn't bathed in over two days. But, even with my friends armed and ready inside the doors of the apartment, I couldn't shut the shower curtain all the way. I had to be able to see the door, had to be able to see if someone was coming for me. In fact, I wouldn't shut the shower curtain for the next twelve months.

Many years later when a friend asked why I didn't give them the drugs, how I wasn't afraid, I told her, "I was afraid. But to give them the meth would have made me disposable. That, or it would have told them that any time they needed drugs they could kidnap or coerce me. Better to take a chance the first time. Better to place my bets while I still had some good cards in my hand. Moxie or insanity. I'm not sure what it was. Something. The will to live, the will to fight. I had no intention of giving them even a line.

They didn't find me again. That night or ever. Maybe they set somebody else up and got their meth elsewhere. Maybe they knew they wouldn't find me unarmed again. Maybe they knew I had connections with the Mexican drug cartel, and they didn't want to get mixed up with that.

Whatever the case, I'd squeezed my way out of another disaster. I'd later learn that that biker group was not playing. A friend told me that months before they'd kidnapped me, they had tortured somebody else—shot battery acid through his veins just because he owed them money. I was lucky. I was often lucky even when it seemed that my life was the unluckiest place in the world.

A WEEK LATER I SHOWED UP AT MY DAUGHTER'S FOSTER home for Christmas. I was still bruised from the beating and had used a ton of concealer and foundation to try to hide it.

Maybe I did from my daughter, but Sabra pulled me over and said, "What happened to you?"

I started to cry. I loved Sabra. I trusted her. But I did not tell her the whole story. Somebody punched me; that was all.

I continued to have my weekly contact with Phoebe at her foster family's house, but when the next holiday came up, and I prepared to go for an extra trip, the social worker—that horrid Jan Ketchel—told me I couldn't go.

"What do you mean?" I asked. "They always let me come for the holidays."

"Well, now they've decided it's best for you not to come for every holiday anymore."

I didn't ask. I didn't push myself on them. But I realized I'd been tattled on. I still had my regular visitation, but there were no more holidays or extra outings. I resented Sabra for this. When I should have loved her more. She was protecting my daughter—protecting her from the drama and harm that I could bring to her life. But protecting her, too, from what Sabra must have seen as inevitable—the time when the state would declare me unfit, the time when Phoebe would be put up for adoption and given to another family for forever.

Soon after my botched visit with Phoebe, I hired two permanent bodyguards. One was another user who was willing to help me out, and the other was a connection from Hawaii. He didn't use, but had an active warrant for his arrest in Hawaii. He was hoping to run before they found him. I sent him a plane ticket, and he was in San Diego within days. After that they were with me for several months, making sure I was safe, trying to make sure I was happy, especially my Hawaiian friend, Po. The fact is that I was often unhappy, angry, stressed. Every time I got bent out of shape, Po would tell me in his soft, singsong accent, "Calm down, sista. Don't worry, don't stress. I hate to see you upset. Why you so upset, sista?"

I never did find out why anyone had a warrant out for Po, but both of my bodyguards got arrested before I did. The cops had come to my apartment looking for me, but found only the two men. I felt horrible. Each of them was shipped off to the jail or prison where he belonged. And soon enough the cops found me.

---

1. Many users will trade their food stamps for drugs. But it's not a very lucrative trade. Most dealers ask for food stamps valued at least twice as much as the worth of the drugs they're selling. In short, for four hundred dollars worth of food stamps, you could buy two hundred dollars worth of drugs. Still, users did it all the time; and gladly.
2. Yes, it sounds like a line from a B-movie, but that's really what they said.
3. The dictionary definition, if you'd like to know, is this: 1) A person's buttocks, 2) A suitcase, bag, or box for carrying possessions or merchandise. Both definitions fit Biker Laura's meaning just fine.
4. Fun fact: Guns are scary, but for me knives have always been worse. They hurt more.
5. I knew it would be empty, but I acted surprised when no one was there.
6. Note to you younger folks who've never used pagers. When you use a pager, you send a number on it. If the recipient knows who you are, he'll call back. In truth, my supplier and I had a little code that we could also send to each other so that the other would know it was them paging, even if the number was unfamiliar, but the biker gang didn't need to know that.

CHAPTER FOURTEEN

I was arrested many times, got stuck in the stinky holding cell, got bailed out, failed to show up in court, had people come look for me (including the U.S. Marshalls), and so on and so forth. Many times. The truth is they don't really want you in jail. They want you to stop doing drugs, stop selling drugs, get a job, but they don't have a good way to make this happen or even help it along. Because of this, the legal system is, to be perfectly honest, a stupid and inefficient system. It's a system where the police work so hard to arrest people, to create a sense of safety and justice in the community, only to let most of those people go, free to show up at court or not until they get caught again.

Efficient or not, the more times you get caught the harder it becomes to get out of jail because your bail keeps getting higher and higher.

Eventually, you get caught and no one can pay it.

That day, for me, was early in 1994. On that day—the day I got arrested for real—I was at my supplier's house when the police kicked in the door. There were always people at my supplier's house—always eight or so guys hanging around, protecting the drugs.

I hadn't shown up for court. The cops had checked every contact. And someone had let them know where to find me. They'd popped the security door open in seconds. We'd been in the bathroom, trying to flush drugs down the toilet. Now everybody was on the floor. A gun pointed at my head and every other head of every other person in the room. These weren't Barbie guns either. They were big rifles. I remember lying on the floor, having a gun pointed at my temple, the cop's foot on my back. He told me, "Don't even think about moving."

I only had two ounces of meth on me, but I also had about eight thousand dollars cash. The cops took it all.[1]

My bail was set at forty thousand dollars this time. And they didn't let me out. I had an FTA—Failure to Appear—for a felony. This meant that I had to be seen by the judge before I could be bailed out. Usually when this happens and you go to see the judge, he'll lower your bail. But not for me. Each time I saw the judge, my bail went up.

I went back to court every few weeks—my legs in shackles, my hands cuffed to another inmate while I rode the county jail bus, passing restaurants I used to love, passing the street I used to take to go out to Sabra's house to visit Phoebe, passing all the freedoms that were now out of my reach.

The longer my stay, the more visits to the judge, the higher my bail became (topping out at fifty-five thousand dollars). The truth is, I'm not sure why. I'm not sure if it's because I'd gotten caught with my supplier, or because I had skipped court before.

All I knew was that the increasing bail amount made me mad. I couldn't pay it. My supplier was in jail with me so he couldn't pay it. The bail bondsman called my dad—with me on the three-way call—to ask if he would be willing to put his house up for collateral. To which my dad replied, "That's not something I can do right now." So polite. So diplomatic. Not even the "Holy no" that the request deserved. But I was angry. Furious. And hurt. My dad and I had been so close. I'd paid to send him and my stepmother to Hawaii, hired a limo to pick him up at the airport, rolled out the red carpet for him. For New Year's Eve, I'd rented a Rolls Royce and bought them a four hundred dollar dinner, then given him and my stepmom an extra trip so they could be alone for a few days. Later, I'd sent him to Vegas to meet me for his birthday. I'd tried to do the best for my dad. He'd loved me so much. Now, he couldn't cough up a little money for me. I couldn't believe that he wouldn't help me get out of jail. I couldn't believe that he thought I would not show up when his butt was on the line. I mean, of course, I wouldn't let him down. Wasn't that obvious?

No. No, it was not obvious. If you're reading this and you're not addicted to drugs, and you've never known someone addicted to drugs, then you can probably see why my dad wouldn't put his house up for collateral for the daughter who had managed to twist her life into a series of debts and court dates, illegal activities and foster care for her child. You can see it, but I couldn't. I really couldn't. The truth was that, at this point, I was afraid of losing Phoebe, and I saw my dad's refusal to get me out of jail as a sign of his lack of love for both me and my child. Sure, she was in foster care. Sure, I was screwing things up and not exactly coming closer to getting her back. But if I landed myself in prison for three years, if I took myself too far away for too long, they would put Phoebe up for adoption, and she would leave my life permanently. Didn't my dad care?

In jail I never got to see Phoebe. Sabra didn't bring her

and I was glad. I did *not* want Phoebe to see me there, wearing my jail blues. Sabra *did* accept the collect calls that I occasionally made. She let me keep as much contact as possible with my daughter. I appreciated that, and was careful not to abuse the privilege. I only called occasionally—every week or two, and talked with Phoebe for a few minutes so that the cost would not become prohibitive to Sabra.

Because of our otherwise limited contact, I wrote Phoebe a lot of letters while I was in jail, letters promising things would change and I would get her back, letters filled with fictions and fantasies that were just as much for my benefit as they were for hers. "I love coffee, I love tea, I love Phoebe, She loves me."

Letters to Phoebe from jail

And she did love me. And I did love her. More than anything. But I didn't know how to build the bridge that would connect my feelings to my actions. And so I continued to write her letters full of all the good intentions that marked my steady path through the hell that had become my life. A stamp was a cheap price to pay for a package of pretty promises. And we all made them. I'm not sure I ever met a parent in jail who didn't promise her children up and down that everything would be different just as soon as she got out. She'd get a new job, a little apartment, buy slippers and read the newspaper for fun.

We all wrote letters to the ones we loved, the ones we let down. We all believed, as our pens hit the page, that we really would change for our families, someday, somehow. We believed we really would pull ourselves together, get jobs, go to Disneyland. We believed this even as we pined for the day we could get out of jail and do a line again, smoke a cigarette, have a drink. We wanted, honestly, to have our cake and eat it too—to be great, responsible parents while feeding our addictions. We wanted what we couldn't have. And so, most of the time, we chose the easiest path of those two. Which was *not* to be great, responsible parents.

My graduation from the holding cell landed me in F house. Which sounds like a censored swear word. Truthfully, F house was the best place to be. F house was the most relaxed incarceration, a lot like a dorm. You had a roommate, but could hang out as a group in the common areas—talking, writing, watching TV. As soon as my bail hit fifty thousand dollars, however, I was moved to B house. B house was for the more hardened criminals and apparently, as someone worth fifty grand, my escape risk was greater as was the loss for the state if I got away. In B house, we were assigned to a room with one roommate. Each night (and a lot of other times as well) we were locked into our rooms.

While in jail, my leg grew increasingly worse. After the break and my surgery, I had never received any follow up care. And now, in jail, my leg was starting to give me some pretty serious problems. The bone was so weak that it began to look like my lower leg was bending, as though it was made of rubber and bowing outward. It was swollen all the time, the ankle easily twice its normal size. Additionally, three of the screws on the top of my foot near the ankle were loosening and creating problems. Since the jail was out in the boonies in southern California, there was dirt and dust everywhere. If a person came into the jail with any shoes other than tennis shoes, the state took her shoes and issued a pair of raggedy old socks and what we called shower shoes. Shower shoes were a pair of cheap plastic flip flops with two straps that went over the top of your foot. Like soccer slides from the dollar store.

Because of the dust and dirt and shower shoes, our feet were always dirty. This wasn't fun for anyone, but for me, with my screwed together cyber-foot, it was especially bad.

I had begun to notice that the screws were almost pushing out of my foot. One was near the inside of my ankle, which was the most sensitive part of my foot. I could see the metal through my skin—a purplish dot as the head of the screw got nearer and nearer to the surface of my skin. And then one day the screw popped out. As in, the literal screw came out of the literal skin of my literal ankle. The nurse in the women's unit of the prison put on a literal Band-Aid. It was all she had.

Consequently, I had to be sent to the men's prison to get medical attention. Going to the men's prison was sort of enviable. When you got there, you felt—even with your prison clothes and gimpy foot—like the most beautiful woman in the world. All the men would watch you and scream, "Hey baby, what's up?" But other than being made to feel cute by fellow felons, I didn't get much from the men's prison. The techs did X-Rays and took other tests that they would send to a doctor for a consultation. A month later, I went back again. They couldn't do anything. At the time, they didn't have a surgery that would fix it, and anything they might try was expensive and probably wouldn't work.

So I got a pair of crutches. Maybe you're thinking, "Well, that must have been kind of good. She probably got some extra attention, maybe she didn't have to work as hard, and who cares about skipping morning exercise." Those crutches were a *curse* in prison. I had to have them all the time and they were considered a deadly weapon.[2] This meant that I was considered dangerous. I would be forced to move out of B Housing and into A Housing.

That was bad.

A Housing was for murderers, rapists, dangerous arsonists. It was a place of complete segregation. Because it was segregated, it was also the place for informants—"snitches"—all those who were willing to tattle on others to reduce their own sentences. The snitches needed the segregation of A Housing because, frankly, everyone else wanted to kill them. Prison can tolerate a lot of types, but informants are not one of them.

I did not want to go to A Housing. I did not want people thinking I was there tattling on them, working with the police. But the things I wanted did not concern the authorities. I went to A Housing, got my yellow bracelet, and they locked me into my single cell, segregated from everybody else's cell.

Often, my crutches and I went to the infirmary to get my leg checked. It was there that I met Deputy Tilman. I was waiting, in terrible pain, to see the nurse so that I could get hooked up with some Motrin or Tylenol—the most powerful painkillers you got in jail. Deputy Tilman was sitting at his desk, watching me and the six or so other girls who were in the waiting room. I remember him leaning back, hands behind his head just like this was some cliché scene from a cop movie.

He looked at me, at us, and said, "Every one of you girls is the same. You come in here, and you're scared to death. But you keep coming back. I see you over and over. Then I don't see you for a while. But it's not because you've cleaned up or gotten a job. It's because you're in the state pen. Then after a few years you get out. And you get arrested again and then I see you again. I've been here for a long time. You're all the same. They should just take you all to a prison island like lepers, and then throw away the key. The state is wasting its money and time trying to change you."

His words were meant to hurt us, maybe to shake us up, maybe make us think, but mostly to hurt us. And they did. At least they hurt me. Looking back, I think that was a good thing. If they hadn't hurt, it would have meant not only that I kind of believed them to be true, but also that in believing I had given up. There must have been some deep part of me that thought he was wrong, that thought, "Of course I have a chance to change, to become something different than what I am right now. Of course, the rest of my life isn't going to be drugs, jail, repeat." But at the time, I didn't think any of that. At the time, I only hurt. And when I hurt, I mouthed off.

Deputy Tilman was a Jew. So naturally I said to him, "I haven't heard such wise words since Hitler." That hit the spot.

He stood up right away. "That's it, Findlay. I've had enough of you. Lockdown." He was so mad, his hands shaking.

Of course I couldn't stop talking. "Thank goodness," I said. "I wanted to be on lockdown. I need to get some sleep. It's like a non-stop party in here."

Deputy Tilman was furious. He picked up his radio and

when he did he dropped his keys—I can still see his hand shaking on his radio. "Lockdown, Findlay, lockdown."

Lockdown usually meant that a fight had broken out, that people needed to be separated because they were violent or out of control. This time, there was just me—running my mouth and comparing a Jewish cop to Hitler. I considered his crazy reaction a sort of win. But it wasn't really. Especially when he probably went home to his family and I went into lockdown and then A House. Without my Tylenol.[3]

No roommates.[4] No windows to the outside world. Just my crutches, my pain, and Roxanne.

Roxanne.

It's not the name of some sexy, helpful drug someone slipped into my cell. Roxanne was the woman in the cell next to mine. When I had first come to A House and walked past Roxanne's room, I'd looked into the tiny window at her door. Roxanne had been in the center of her cell. Her hair was blond, curly, completely wild—like a human animal. The floor of her cell was covered with old food, spit, waste. Most of us in A House at least looked forward to our meals. It was all we had. Roxanne's meals had to be slid in to her through a special slot. And then when she got that food, she would pick up the plate and throw it at the window—all the food splattered against yesterday's food and the food from the days before that. Onto these layers of food, she would spit and smear feces. And then she'd take up howling.[5]

Roxanne howled all night long—screaming, spitting, stomping, wailing. Everything echoed. She kept me awake most of the night. She kept many of us awake most of the night. The guards would try to calm her down, but it didn't help. I mean, what were they going to do, give her a Tylenol?

Years later, when I finally cracked a Bible I would find Roxanne in its pages—different body, different setting, same life. A man in the desert, possessed by devils, living in the wilderness and running around naked, tearing his skin, screaming, crying[6]. I don't know what Legion of demons was in Roxanne's head, but I do know that there was no Jesus hanging out in A House to remove them. At least not directly.

There was a guard—Gutierrez. He was a nice guy. In truth, there were plenty of jerks in law enforcement, but there were plenty of nice guys too. Not that we liked them, not that we appreciated the good work they did, day in and day out. Nope. We hated them all. But looking back, I remember them —names and faces. Looking back I thank them for being kind and unjaded in a world that almost demanded a certain amount of hardness. One night when Roxanne wouldn't stop screaming, Gutierrez just started singing. He had a nice voice and there was really nothing else to do. Gently, almost sweetly, he sang a song from the '70s, "Roxanne, you don't have to put on that red dress." It didn't help Roxanne; she screamed on. But, looking back, I think it helped me—to see a piece of the good, a taste of the sweet, among so much bitter.

---

1. This is standard. When you are arrested for drug dealing, all of your money is taken, as well as any possessions you have. This is because the law assumes everything has been stolen unless you can somehow prove it was not (you can't). On the one hand, this makes perfect sense: Why should you be allowed to keep the money or goods that shouldn't have been yours in the first place? On the other hand, it puts every dealer who leaves jail penniless and homeless in a tricky position. What is the one thing they can do to make some money really quick so they can get some food, clothes, and a place to stay? The answer is, obviously, *not* to attend several job interviews until they, with their felony records, are finally hired by a fine establishment such as Burger Biz, only to receive their first paycheck of ninety-five dollars two weeks later. No, the thing that usually happens is that people start

selling drugs again—almost as soon as their ride screeches out of the jail parking lot.

2. When they told me this, I replied with classic humility and cooperation, "Well, my mind's a deadly weapon too, but you never punished me for that."

3. Years later, when I was clean and went back to the court house to pay a fine, I saw Deputy Tilman again as I was walking out of the court house. "Hey Deputy Tilman," I yelled. "Remember me? You told me I was going to prison and I didn't. I turned my life around and here I am." Right away, I called my dad, triumphant. My dad must have been smiling when he said, "See, that's the best revenge. Success." I guess I shouldn't have been worried about revenge at all, but I'll tell you this—calling to Deputy Tilman from across the street as a totally free woman felt a whole lot better than mouthing off before being forced to hobble back to my jail cell on crutches.

4. Later I did get a roommate—a Hispanic woman who had killed her boyfriend/husband. A murderer. For the record, she was always really quiet, calm, and sweet with me.

5. Roxanne should not have been in A Housing. Roxanne should not have been anywhere but a mental institution where she might have gotten some of the care and medicine she needed.

6. St. Mark 5:1-5

CHAPTER FIFTEEN

Everyone wants to get out of jail early. But no one wants to get out of jail early for the reason I did.

One week I called my daughter, as I occasionally did. Usually, we talked about her school, what she'd been up to, how proud I was of her, and of course, how everything was going to be better when I got out.

This time when I called, we didn't get to any of that. Because this time, Phoebe started out by saying, "Oh, Mom, I'm so sorry about Uncle Robert."

My baby brother—the one I loved so much. "Why? What happened to Uncle Robert?"

Phoebe—nine years old, in foster care for the last 2 ½ years, her mother in jail—that little girl paused on the other end of the line, another burden suddenly on her shoulders. "Well," she said after a minute. "He died."

I didn't listen, couldn't listen. "This must be a mistake," I told her.

Of course it had to be a mistake. Otherwise I would have heard. Someone would have called me. Shouldn't I have gotten an official letter from the jail or someone, somewhere? [1]

I called my dad. My sweet stepmom answered and I asked her what had happened to Robert. She paused and then said, "Let me get your dad."

My dad got onto the phone, "What happened?" I demanded. "What happened to Robert?"

My father couldn't even speak. He began to cry—huge choking man sobs. "My baby boy, my baby boy. My beautiful baby boy." [2]

Robert had gone on a small plane with a couple of friends —flown over the San Francisco Bay. They had lost contact with air traffic control, never returned.

"They'll find the plane," I told my dad. "They'll find Robert."

I was in the first stages of my denial, but my father had been all through his. "No," he said, "it's been too many days."

Later, they would find the body of one of my brother's friends. It wasn't nearly enough closure, and it was no consolation at all. But it's all we got.

I was crying now. My dad still sobbing.

I went back to my cell, inconsolable. I cried hysterically until I fell asleep—it felt like passing out—and then I woke up and cried some more. For days, I cried and cried until I fell into the unconsciousness of sleep. And then I would wake up and cry again.

I wasn't quite Roxanne, but the staff was worried about me. I was supposed to be released in several weeks anyway. The chaplain arranged it so I could get out earlier for a "compassionate release."

I got out, a friend picked me up, and I did a line and had a cigarette. My heart wasn't in it, but my body appreciated the pick up.

My dad and my brother Randy sent money so I could get a hotel and go to Robert's memorial service in Elko, Nevada. I spent all the money. I had no food, no real shoes, only a small box of clothes an old roommate had saved for me in his garage. I had no quick fix for my problems or my sadness, and so I did a few lines and drank a lot. I'm sure I rationalized that if I used that money to feel better, I would be able to get some more from somewhere else.

I did. After I spent all my money, my dad and brother bought me a plane ticket that would be waiting for me at the counter at the airport. And so I made my way to Nevada.

It was there that I saw my mom again. I hadn't spoken to her in 3 ½ years. She threw her arms around me crying, "You're my baby now."

Inside I felt as cold as ice. I was still mad that she had pressured me to send Phoebe to be with the uncle who abused her; I was still furious that she had written a letter stating I was an unfit mother. I was still blaming her for the mounds of problems that had beset my life. Still, I let her hug me and after that, we began to speak again.

I was in Nevada for five days. My brother Randy lived there with his wife and kids. I stayed at his house, sleeping most of the time—the result of coming down after my post-jail meth use. When I wasn't sleeping, I went out to the garage to smoke cigarettes so Randy's kids wouldn't see me. Soon after I arrived, Randy came out and asked me, "Where have you been for the last four years?"

Four years.

The number smacked me in the face even more than the question. I had no idea how long it had been. At the time, if you'd asked me how long it had been since I'd spoken to or visited my older brother, I wouldn't have been able to tell you. It felt like months, though I must have known it was more.

Until I moved to California, I'd gone to visit my brothers twice every year. Each year when I came to the mainland to visit my parents, I would also fly to whatever state Randy was living in and visit him, Robert, and my oldest brother Donnie. It hadn't been a lot of contact, but it had been very steady contact. And then, one day, I was gone. *Where have you been for the last four years?* It was an impossible question to answer. I had been everywhere, and nowhere. I had been to hell and back to hell again. I had been in dozens of apartments, in fancy hotels, in jail cells, in cars I didn't own, in apartments where I didn't belong. I had gone around in circles, a child spinning until she fell down, only to stand back up and do it again. And I had been doing it for four years. I still could not get over the amount of time. Where had it gone? Time without seeing my mother. Time without speaking to my brothers. Time I couldn't get back, time I couldn't even calculate. But Randy knew. Four years. Spinning, dizzy.

"I tried to call you," Randy said. "We tried to find you, but we never could."

FOR THE MEMORIAL SERVICE, THERE WAS NO BODY, NO ASH, just us and a jumble of memory and loss crashing together. I sat by my niece, who was maybe nine years old. She was sobbing hysterically. All of Randy's kids were—dressed in their Sunday best, and crying right along with the adults. Robert had been close with Randy's family—living with them for his last year of high school when our parents had been going through a divorce, making an apartment in Randy's basement and working in Nevada.

My father went up to speak, his bottom lip shaking the entire time. Then Randy spoke briefly. He said that Robert always knew how to work really hard. Work hard and play hard. It was true. I missed Robert so much that I couldn't believe he was gone. Everyone else had come to grips with his loss, but I was still in denial, hoping he would turn up in some hospital in San Francisco with amnesia. After all, they hadn't found his body or the plane. But everyone else knew he was gone. They'd had more time to deal with it than me; and perhaps more importantly, they'd spent their time dealing with it, not doing a line every time the feelings got too hard.

After the funeral, when we were all cried out, I went home and slept some more.

When I *was* awake, my family saw how bad my leg had become. It was swollen to twice its natural size, screws through the skin, the bone weak and bowed. "You need to see a doctor," they told me. But I didn't have any money or insurance. I didn't even have an apartment to live in.

My dad said, "You need to put in for social security, then go to the university hospital. They take low-income patients." But I knew that if I showed up with any drugs in my urine, no doctor on earth would help me. Why would they help a woman who was taking a drug that weakened and destroyed her bones? Even if they took charity patients, they would first care for others—those who needed help just as much as I did, and who weren't doing a drug that would destroy all the effort the doctors might exert helping me save my bones.

Still, with the loss of my brother, the jail time, the crippling in my leg, something inside me seemed to break.

Or maybe it fixed.

For the first time since I started dealing, I wanted to be done, to step back, to get away. I still had no money, no job, no skills, no physical ability to stand for any period of time. When I returned to California, I would have nowhere to stay except with friends. Friends who did drugs—the only friends I had, the only people I knew. When I returned to California, I would have no work to do, except to sell drugs, of course. Except that the *of course* just wasn't there anymore. I wanted out. Somehow.

A few weeks later, Phoebe's foster mother called me. "Laura. It's been three years. Soon they're going to put her up for adoption." Adoption. Because my daughter deserved a stable life in a stable home with someone who could be counted on to be there for her for the rest of her life.

Often alcoholics and drug addicts talk about their rock bottom moment—the day they woke up in an unfamiliar hotel room with a drunk woman draped across their legs. Or the time they found themselves in the hospital with almost all their teeth knocked out. Or the morning they woke up with blood between their legs and didn't know why. I didn't have any of these moments. What I had was much simpler. A younger brother who died when it should have been me.

And a daughter I was about to lose. Not dead, but vanished from my life. Which felt like almost the same thing.

A stable life in a stable home with someone who could be counted on to be there for her for the rest of her life.

I realized then that that needed to be me. I'd lost enough. I wanted my daughter back.

I WAS STILL A TRAIN WRECK THOUGH.

It would have made for a better story if I had simply resolved to step away from drugs and then left with some grand gesture. But I didn't. The leap was so big, the chasm so wide. And so, I should be clear that even with my new resolve, I wasn't totally clean. I was still using meth occasionally, though I knew I would need to quit and knew I was taking a big risk. I was still living with my old friends, who were doing drugs. This was also a big risk. If someone had reported them, if a cop had come in and found us, I would have been caught, caught while on probation. And this time if I got caught, I would skip jail and make my way to the four-year commitment that was prison. It was a risk I took since there was nothing else to do, nowhere else to go. But I wasn't selling it anymore, refused all my friends who kept trying to draw or drag me back in. With one exception.

My friend, Art, was trying to get rid of some of his supply. We had met about a year earlier during a different drug transaction and had become friends, occasionally hanging out or doing a line together. He knew I had good drug connections and he wanted me to help move some of his supply along.

"Nope," I told him. "I'm getting out of it. I'm getting my daughter back."

"If you don't want to sell any weight, alright, then just make a couple of moves for me so I can get money back to my people."

It was a favor. I never could turn down a favor. And he wasn't exactly asking me to sell, just to help him sell. Fine. I agreed to find two buyers—one for a half ounce, one for a quarter ounce. For that, Art would give me a quarter ounce as profit. It seemed easy enough. And it would benefit me as well.

I was still barely out of jail and didn't have a car, so Art and his cousin, who I didn't know, agreed to give me a ride. I made a couple of transactions and unloaded the drug, then went back into his van, asking for my quarter ounce.

I'd just taken a huge risk for this guy, a risk I shouldn't have taken, a risk that could have lost me the new life I kept catching glimpses of in my peripheral vision, but couldn't quite seem to get into focus. I just wanted a little of the drug he owed me. Which was actually really dumb too, but as I said, I was dirt poor, not completely clean, and I definitely, definitely did not always play the smartest cards.

This was no exception. But it doesn't end how you might think. Art was high. Not only that, he'd been high for days and hadn't slept at all. This wasn't uncommon. Unfortunately, when you get to that point—awake and high for days—you often start to feel paranoid, worried, haunted, illogical, violent. You begin to think everyone around you is out to get you. This is what happened to Art.

"Can I get my quarter ounce now," I asked, flopping into the passenger seat and pulling out a cigarette.

"What are you talking about?" Art said, buggy-eyed, red-faced.

"My quarter ounce," I said. "My share for unloading your drugs."

"What are you trying to pull," he said, his voice rising, hands jittery.

"I'm not jeopardizing my butt for nothing," I said. "I want my quarter ounce." (Remember that part about me not always playing the best cards. I also didn't always choose to play them at the right times.)

Art got mad, started cursing, flipping out. "I thought we were friends," he said.

"What are you talking about?" I shouted. "I'm not risking jail time to sell this for nothing."

"I don't know what you're trying to pull," he said again. And this time he whipped out a nine millimeter gun and cocked it, just like that. "What the hell are you trying to pull?"

What flashed through my mind was that this was what I was going to give my daughter, that this was what she would have to remember me by—my brains blown up against the side of a van.

Art pressed the gun against my neck, pushing my head against the van door, cursing.

His cousin was in the back. "Whoa, bro, keep it cool, keep it cool," he said to Art. And then to me, "Don't worry about it. Don't worry about it. He's just been up too long."

Yeah, sure, what was I worried about? Just the gun digging a bruise into my neck, and my own friend too crazy to realize what he was doing.

"You don't want to do this," his cousin pleaded. "We just need to get out of here."

"She's trying to rip me off," Art screamed.

"No, come on, man. It's cool. Let's just go before the cops come."

Eventually, after what seemed like years, but must have only been a minute, Art's cousin coaxed and pleaded him down, and Art put the gun away, though he was still angry. I got out of the van. I wanted to be sure to leave while he was calm enough to let me go. I didn't ask again for my quarter ounce.

A few months later, I saw Art at a convenience store, and he apologized, as though we had just had a little disagreement over who was paying for dinner. "Sorry," he said. "I don't know what happened. We're, like, homies, right?" He wanted to come and hang out, get high and watch movies.

Nope. I'd almost lost that game and I wasn't going to risk it again.

In a strange way, almost getting my head shot off was

good for me. If all had gone smoothly, if I'd gotten my quarter ounce, and then sold it to make a little money, then it would have been easy—so terribly easy—to slide right back into that old life, the habits I knew, the business I knew. As it was, not only did I have no meth to sell, but I also had Art's furious, high, paranoid face flashing through my memory. This guy who had been my friend had flipped on me, had been ready to kill me. Even worse, he couldn't quite seem to realize that. He had been too high to sleep, too high to think, way too high to care.

It was time, I knew, to move away from my old crowd. I worried that if I didn't I would never be able to move away from the drug life that encircled me, caged. But moving away wasn't easy. Not because I wasn't ready. Not because I didn't see the importance. But because I had no money, no job, and a very serious criminal record.

I CALLED MY BROTHER, RANDY, IN NEVADA AND ASKED IF I could stay with him and his family—live in his basement apartment like Robert had. It made sense to me. I needed to be away from my friends, from the drugs and drug culture that I'd so carefully built up around myself. And I could pay Randy rent; that would help him out. Randy had a big house with a huge basement apartment where Robert had been living for a while. I would help Randy a little with bills and he would help me a little with life.

Randy, however, wasn't so sure that his house with four rambunctious kids was the right place for his drug-head, jail-bird sister. Still, he didn't say no right away. If I'd had my head on straight, I might have appreciated that. I didn't quite. Not yet. When Randy came back to me with an, "I'm sorry. I just can't put anything more on my wife right now," I was mad.

Besides, I thought, it wasn't like I would be a burden to them. It's not as if I would be *put* on his wife, Jackie. As if I wasn't an adult who could take care of herself. Except, wait, I wasn't. When I'd stayed at their house for the funeral, coming down from the high I'd helped myself to before coming to Nevada, I'd slept through every spare moment. Once Jackie had asked me to watch my two youngest nephews while she ran to the store. "Sure," I'd said. When she got back, I was dead asleep on the couch and the boys had colored with marker all over the playhouse they'd been playing in.

Still, I was furious with my brother. "I need a stable place to live or I can't get Phoebe back," I shouted into the phone. "You've helped everyone else out, but when I ask, you can't help me." After that I cussed him out and slammed down the pay phone I was using.

It was true. He'd helped everyone. He'd built a house for both my dad and my mom. He'd given my little brother a place to stay when he needed it. He'd even helped my older brother, who suffered from a bi-polar disorder and alcoholism. Randy had hooked my older brother up with different jobs, even though that hadn't always gone well. So even though Randy was willing to be embarrassed over and over by our older brother, even though he was willing to sweat and stress for everyone else, he couldn't do a thing for me.

Now I would be stuck trying to stay sober while living with other addicts, sleeping on their couches, and watching their kids for a few hours to pay for my presence. I felt betrayed. I felt like no one cared enough to help me get my daughter back.

I couldn't see what Randy must have seen. I couldn't

understand the reasons he and Jackie might have been afraid to take their drug addict sister into their house with their four small children. Even if I had managed to stay clean, I still smoked almost constantly, drank when there were problems, and swore without even thinking. My brother was a Mormon[3] and none of those things was any part of his life, and they certainly weren't influences he wanted on his children.

Besides, there was no guarantee I would stay clean. At this point, I had been addicted to drugs for about thirteen years—longer than any of his kids had been alive. All the statistics were against me. Even among meth addicts who attend rehab, only a slim twelve percent recover. For those who don't get rehab, the number shrinks to a depressing five percent. For those who deal, the number withers to less than one percent[4]. Letting me into his house must have felt like he was chopping the crystals himself.

Now, there was no Randy to whisk me away from my circle, to enable me out of my drug use. Now, I had to want to change badly enough to do it myself.

So the question I had to ask myself was, "Did I?"

Any other time, the answer would have been *No*. Any other time, that would have been the end of it. I would have gone back to dealing, gotten some money, found a place to live.

This time was different. A little bit, which was a lot for me. This time I finally did what my father had told me to do: I applied for social security. Before my drug life, I'd been working for as long as I'd been legally able to do so. Now I had a significant injury. Social security was worth a shot. While I waited to see if I would qualify, I stayed at a friend's house, doing a line occasionally, but mostly trying to stay clean while I waited.

It was a place of limbo for me, a tipsy little point where I wasn't dealing and was trying to cut back on using, but still wasn't completely off of drugs. It was a time when I had no money, and only some tiny threads of hope. I held to those threads with my all and everything.

Everyone warned me that my social security application would probably get rejected the first few times, but through some miracle, mine didn't. When I got approved and got that first check, it was the first time in years that I had money that hadn't been acquired through a crime. It wasn't a lot of money, but it was mine to use legally. Now I just had to get away from my friends.

I knew I needed to leave the area I was in. And I knew what other drug-infested areas and neighborhoods I should avoid. The problem was that the places I wanted to be didn't exactly want to have me. Interestingly, most landlords don't want to rent their apartments to convicted felons with no recent work history, and a serious leg handicap. Go figure.

Fortunately, miraculously, I eventually found a place—a little one-bedroom apartment rented to me by an Afghan couple who owned the liquor store directly below it. This apartment they were willing to rent to a gimpy-legged, non-working felon—it was not the Hilton. In the kitchen alone, there were five different color schemes, though I can't remember what they all were. The refrigerator was avocado green. The counters were a disgusting color that must have once been yellow, but now was just dingy. The linoleum floor was from the '70s, beat up, chipped, and peeling off. It was probably brown. The walls didn't match any of it.

I repainted everything. And by everything, I really mean everything. If it could be painted, it was. I went to the home store and picked out whatever colors were on clearance or had been returned or mixed wrong. I came home with some neutral beiges along with peach, black, and gold. This totally worked in the '90s. I did the kitchen walls in peach, then used a black and peach stick-on border around the top. I used black appliance paint to paint the refrigerator and a special type of paint for the countertops. Most of the knobs for the cupboards were missing, but I found several in the drawers and screwed them in. They were old and cracked. When I painted them over with my black paint, a small amount of the cracked paint showed through, making them look like black lace. It was actually incredibly pretty and went along perfectly with the whole peach and black theme. I used a vinyl roll out floor over the old linoleum.

When I was done, I moved on to the bedroom. The bedroom was small with one cinder block wall, which reminded me of jail. I used gold spray paint to fill in the cracks[5], then rolled over all of it with beige. From the dollar store, I bought strands of plastic ivy leaves. I spray painted them gold and then coiled them against the wall, making it look like a head board. I painted all the doorknobs black.

Now all I needed was some furniture. I scoured the ads in the paper and finally found a bed, armoire, and dresser. The bed was a white and beige platform bed with drawers under-neath. Everything was in excellent condition, but had tarnished gold hardware. I took the furniture home, removed the hardware, and re-painted it gold, so that it looked brand new. When that was done, I bought fake white leather couches for the living room, as well as a palm tree, which I decorated with white Christmas lights.

And I was proud of it—so proud. For the first time in a long, long time, I was proud of what I had done—of the beauty I had created from something ugly. Before when dealing drugs, I had money but still couldn't buy or create the things I'd wanted to. Now I had almost no money, but was making a house, trying to nudge it into a home.[6]

When the landlord saw it, he was shocked. "Is this the same place?" he asked, staring at the rooms. Even Jan Ketchel was impressed when she came by to inspect it.

I'd finally done what they'd told me to do three and a half years earlier—I'd gotten my own place. That was half the battle. Now I just needed to prove to them that I was clean. Staying off drugs was so much easier now that I was away from my drug-using friends. Even so, quitting completely wasn't easy. I was sick. I was tired. But at this point, how can I say that it was exactly hard? Nothing in the last three years had been easy. Dealing drugs, doing drugs, going to jail, trying to get out of jail, ignoring my family, coping with my family. Getting caught, not getting caught. Running the business of selling drugs, keeping this business under the radar. Being threatened at knife point. Being threatened at gun point. It was time-consuming, energy-draining, life threatening; it was *hard*.

Now, no one had cause to rip me open with a machete. Now, no one needed to pull me over and slam me to the ground, handcuffing me behind my back. Now, no one had reason to shove my head against the window of a van, holding a gun to my neck, about to pull the trigger. So, yeah, quitting was hard. But compared to the life I'd been living, it wasn't *that* hard.

Usually people on probation got a drug test once a week. My old friends had told me all kinds of ways I could get around the pee tests—where I could get fake pee, how I could sneak it in. I didn't. Instead, I told my probation officer I wanted to be tested twice a week. I didn't want to be tempted, didn't want to think I could evade the drug test by getting high the day after they gave it to me, didn't want to take a chance. I wanted some accountability. I wanted enough accountability to keep me clean. The powers that be, through the voice of Jan Ketchel, had warned me that soon they would put Phoebe up for adoption. My time was ticking.

I knew that at this point if I got busted for doing or dealing drugs, it would be a violation of my probation. That meant that I would get about four years in the state prison. If that happened I would lose Phoebe for sure.

So I painted any surface that I could think of, and took more drug tests than I had to.

After I had been clean and living in my apartment for several months Phoebe was allowed to come visit, and then— eventually—to stay overnight. Everything went well. We went back to court. I was told, "You can have her back, but you can't have her there."

After all that work, after the paint and the refurbishing, I found out that the state would require me to have a two-bedroom apartment. They weren't doing it to be difficult. In fact, they helped me apply for benefits for Phoebe so I would have the money for a two bedroom apartment and another bed. This time, I moved up a step from my dive-painted-into-less-of-a-dive apartment. I wanted Phoebe to have a nice place to live. I found a two-bedroom condo with a fireplace in a gated community in Chula Vista. They didn't want to rent it to me because of my small social security check. They said, "There's no way you're going to make it with your income."

I said, "I'll make it. I just need a good apartment." Either they were desperate or some kind of guardian angel whacked somebody on the head because I told them, "I don't care if I have to pinch in other areas; I just want a good place for my daughter." They rented it to me.[7]

As soon as I proved to the court that I had a legitimate income and an apartment with a lease, I got my daughter back. We bought a used dresser. I painted it purple.

Jan Ketchel, the social worker whom I had hated with my

all and everything, stood up in court and said, "I've never seen a mother do so much to get her daughter back. I see mothers all the time who lose their children, then just go out and make another child. It's gut wrenching. It's so good to see a mother try so hard to get her daughter back."

And then, through my non-drug eyes, I saw this woman— overworked and often discouraged, a woman I'd hated because I thought she was against me all the time, a woman who'd really been on my side (and Phoebe's side) all along, who'd really been cheering for me to succeed, to win, when all of my drug addict "friends" had been hoping for a fail, not caring if my daughter came back into my life or had a good life, only caring that I could supply them with their dope, only caring that I would take care of their next high and make it a good one.

---

1. Answer: No. Social services might contact my daughter to let her know her uncle had died. But no such courtesy was extended to the prisoners of the Los Colinas. Even if tax payers had wanted their money to go towards keeping the nation's felons updated on the tales and tragedies that often followed them and their families, it wasn't a realistic possibility. There was no way for the prison to seek out information and/or family news and then report back to us. People could visit, but my family wasn't local. And no one could call in to the jail; we could only call out. Which meant that if someone wanted me to know about Robert, I would have to call them. If I didn't, they would have to write and send me a letter. Even if someone had done that, I hadn't had time to get it.

2. He couldn't speak for minutes. Later, my stepmother told me that the police had offered to remove all the guns in the house (which was somewhat standard in Florida at the time). My dad was so distraught that they had accepted the offer.

3. A member of the Church of Jesus Christ of Latter-day Saints

4. Many are jailed; many die. Some just keep on using and selling. Part of the reason for this is that it's just as hard to give up the money and power as it is the drug itself. I had worked my way up to the point

where I sold larger chunks of drug (which meant I had to see fewer people, which meant it took less time and was just easier). When you can get twenty-five hundred dollars for quarter pound of meth, it's hard to step down and make do on minimum wage working on your feet all day at the 7 Eleven.

5. In Japan, when a piece of pottery is broken, it is sometimes repaired with lacquer mixed with gold (*Kintsugi*), making it even more beautiful and valuable. I did not know this at the time, as I filled those cinder block cracks with discount gold spray paint, but I was doing the same thing.

6. Randy—who was still on my bad list—started calling me almost every day, asking what he could do, if there was a way he could help. I don't really remember if I asked him for help at that point or not, but I do remember realizing that my brother *did* want to help, that he had always wanted to help. The few times it had seemed he was abandoning me had really been times when he was actually just worried about abandoning his own family's safety for me. Once I was off drugs, it became much easier to consider Randy's own worries and fears. No dad wants to risk coming home one day to find his not-quite-recovered addict of a sister cooking up a pot of meth on the stove in the kitchen (p.s. I've never actually cooked meth; it's not quite *Breaking Bad*).

7. With all that penny pinching, we were incredibly broke. Each month, my mom would send us fifty dollars and it felt like a million dollars. We didn't have a phone so Mom got us a phone and had it installed.

CHAPTER SIXTEEN

A nd they all lived happily ever after.
Oh, wait—different story.
Because I was still a single mother living off state support
with a bum leg and a daughter who had been molested by her
uncle, lied to by her mother, taken by the state, and raised in
foster care for the last three years. We all had some pretty
serious growing pains left.

Serious.

Pains.

When Phoebe came into my home, she was happy to be
back. There was no anger at leaving her foster family—only
excitement at being reunited. And I was over the moon. I had
my baby back. I had my life back on course. The problem
was that not being addicted to drugs isn't the only necessary
qualification for parenthood. And I hadn't spent the last few
years of my life reading up on good parenting. Additionally,
Phoebe was carrying a little baggage of her own.

As the months blew by, Phoebe seemed to form into three
different people. First, there was her normal 11-year-old self,
basically happy with normal moods. Second, there was baby

Phoebe—a little girl who would skip into my room like a four-year-old, chirping like a bird and say, "Hi Mommy." This child was sweet, but there was something not quite right, some yearning to rewind all those years, to let go of the burdens her young shoulders had been forced to bear, to be innocent and helpless. And then there was Mob Boss Phoebe. There were the days she would go off like a 20-year-old ex con—defiant, mean, cursing, punching. Over the years, I've patched up more holes in the wall than it seems any mother of one girl should ever have to.

And while, inwardly, I took all the guilt and fault unto myself, outwardly I didn't. Phoebe would get into one of her crazy moods and scream, "It's all your fault. You let me be molested."

Inside, I would be crying. Inside I would believe that I did, that I should have followed my gut, should have seen it, should have kept it from happening. But outwardly, I screamed back, "That wasn't me. That was your dad's sicko family. It's not my fault that your father's side of the family is so messed up." And she'd scream, "Don't talk about my dad."

Or another day, she would scream, "You don't even care about me. Otherwise, you wouldn't have left me in foster care." Of course, I felt beyond guilty for that; of course I felt like the queen of screw up. But instead I screamed back, "I've been busting my butt trying to get you back. I love you more than anything or I would have just gone and made another baby and forgotten about you."

In a lot of ways, living with Phoebe through those years was like living with an alcoholic parent. We'd fight in terrible, horrible ways—both of us screaming, Phoebe slamming doors, punching walls, breaking things that would have to be repaired. Then, a few hours later, she would come to my room and say, "I'm sorry. You know I love you."

I did.

Still the arguments continued. Still they escalated.

And on we went. I didn't know how to validate my child's feelings and help her heal. I didn't know how to validate my own feelings and heal. I didn't know how to stop the arguments or keep them from happening. I didn't know that if I let go of my side of the rope, there could be no tug of war.

And so we battled forward. I was terrified to tell anyone I needed help. If Phoebe had to get counseling or go in for mental problems, I was afraid that they would consider me unfit and take her away from me again. And so the holes in my wall kept getting patched. And so the dressers and mirrors and lamps kept getting fixed or replaced.

And then one day she got mad and tried to jump out of the car while I was driving. We were going at least thirty-five miles per hour. Losing her to foster care again was almost the worst thing I could think of. But losing her because she died in a fit of rage or rebellion or self-destruction was even worse. I took her to the psychiatric hospital.

She was there for a few days, and then she came back and we were okay for a bit before we started up again. At that time, there was no family counseling, no real follow up; at least there was none that I can remember.[1] Our social worker checked on us to make sure things looked okay. They did, and that was that.

SEVERAL MONTHS AFTER RECEIVING STATE AID, I WAS ABLE TO get my leg taken care of. Which makes it sound easier than it was. The bone had begun to deteriorate and would, in fact, need to be re-grown.

Re-grown.

The bone was bent inward and crooked, the ankle swollen to the size of a softball all the time, hot to the touch, inflamed and red. Only Dr. Peter Newton at UC San Diego would even try. Everyone else wanted to amputate. The situation with my leg was so complicated—so many nerves, so much liability. Cutting it off seemed like the easiest thing. My dad told me, "Don't you let them." I didn't want to, but the truth was that if Dr. Newton hadn't been willing to take me on as a patient, I wouldn't have had any other options.[2]

In order to re-grow my leg, Dr. Newton and his team first had to cut out two inches of bone from my ankle. The bone was deformed and infected, something they didn't know until they actually went in to do surgery. When I came out of surgery, they told me, "We had to cut a lot of infected bone out of your leg."[3] Now one leg was shorter than the other. In order to correct this significant discrepancy, the doctors were going to try to regrow my leg. It was a new, experimental procedure. Bone, even when not connected to other bone, can grow. So if they could immobilize my leg in a type of brace, holding it in position with just a hair of space between the bones, the bones would grow toward one another. This is essentially what happens when a bone is broken in a normal way—they set it and it grows together again.

In my case however, there was a lot more bone than usual that needed to be grown. Because of this, the bones—even as they were growing towards one another—would need to be pulled, micrometer by micrometer, away from each other. In this way the bone would continue to grow, and over time would be restored.

Growing back that leg was a lot like growing back my life. Slow. Excruciating. My foot and leg were run through with wires. The wires began just above my toes. They ran through the arch of my foot into skin and all the way through to the other side. A similar pattern was repeated up my leg to the knee.

Did you catch that? There were basically wires woven through my skin all the way up to my knee. The metallic, brace-like contraction that surrounded my leg, holding everything in place was called an ilizarov, or outer fixation. Wire rings held the whole thing together while smaller wires shot through and around my leg and foot. Frankensteinian. The wires latched on with pins to the ankle. There were screws on the device on my ankle and all up my leg. Every six hours[4] I was supposed to turn those screws with a small wrench, and it would stretch my leg out just the tiniest bit more. In a way, it was similar to how braces work. Gradually, over time, you pull the teeth into a different position. Except, unlike braces, I was gradually pulling one part of my bone the smallest distance away from the other part of my bone, in the hope that the bone would grow that tiny amount. Then I'd stretch my leg out again, and the bone would grow into that little bit of empty space, and on and on for months until, if all went well, the bone would grow back the two inches it had lost. No one was promising that it would work. But we all hoped.

At two weeks when I went in for my first x-ray, there was a tiny, but visible growth. The doctors celebrated. Maybe I would have too, except that I hurt too much. I was supposed to put weight onto my foot and leg as soon as possible. But even the smallest pressure on my foot was searing. At first I could barely walk ten steps a day (and by walk, I mean just put my foot down on the ground with the tiniest amount of weight or pressure).

During this time, we lived on the second floor. I had to scoot up the steps on my butt. It was nothing short of completely humiliating. I had to use a motorized scooter at the store. I couldn't drive myself anywhere, so people would give me rides or I would take the bus. I wore long dresses all the time because there was no way to wear pants over the ilizarov.

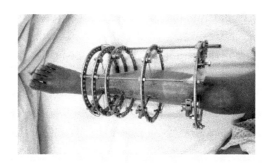

Ilizarov (Note: This is a stock image, not my leg. I hated how my leg looked and took very few pictures of my leg at that time, and none that show the ilizarov as well as this.)

Over the course of the year, in six-hour intervals, we managed to grow that leg back. At the beginning, the skin on my leg couldn't even be closed because it was so swollen. The skin was held together with big fat stiches, and then wrapped with bandages that needed to be changed frequently. When I changed the dressings, I could see the *inside* of my leg. To me it looked like hamburger beef tied together with some thread—a horror movie doll leg.

Even after the bone had grown back, I had to wait for the swelling to go down before my leg could heal the rest of the way. It took at least another month. I wrapped it regularly, caring for it with the anti-bacterial ointment the doctors had given me. And, eventually the swelling went down and the skin began to grow back together over my repaired bone. In a few months, all that remained of my Franken-leg was a scar that ran from my ankle to my knee, pink and raised, strangely numb to the touch.

You know what wasn't numb? The places where the wires had gone through my skin in their amusement park ride around my leg. When the nurse had originally taken the wires out of my leg, I'd gone nuts, screaming, begging her to stop. I'd felt like I was going to pass out. She'd looked at me and said, "Hey, it doesn't hurt *that* bad." I wanted to kill her.[5] Because, for whatever reason, it hurt way more than it should have.

Later testing would show that I had something called reflex sympathetic dystrophy—an "abnormal excitation of nervous tissue, leading to abnormal impulses along nerves that affect blood vessels and skin."[6] It usually comes after a triggering event. A surgery, for example, or maybe having your entire leg run through with wires for almost a year; or how about both. Having a past filled with drugs, and a present filled with smoking, drinking, aspartame, and caffeine probably weren't helping either, though I didn't know that at the time.

In addition to the real pain of healing from such a significant and invasive event, plus the extra pain from my irritated nerves, I also began to fear my pain. This created extra anxiety, and therefore (you guessed it) even more pain—like a child who, afraid of the pain of a shot, feels it so much more intensely than one who either doesn't know it's coming or is brave enough to deal with it.

The most tender part of my leg was the bottom of my foot where the wires had been run through. It was a good two months before the pain started going away. And that was just the beginning.

For another year after the ilizarov came off, I had to wear a plastic mold over my leg. It was like a hard plastic brace. It kept my leg straight. I could wear shoes and baggy pants with it, but I hated it. It was impossibly hot, miserable, restrictive. But I wore it. Because hot, miserable, and restrictive were going to buy me a life of walking on my very own leg.

---

1. I am told that it's standard to have a social worker assigned to Phoebe and I think we did, but I can't remember what she did or how she helped. There definitely wasn't any family counseling for the two of us.
2. Dr. Newton donated time teaching at the hospital. He worked with children who had muscular problems. He took me on as a patient. So, basically, he was a total saint.
3. Why was it infected? I don't know. Probably from a combination of drug use, lack of follow up care, and the dingy conditions my leg was in as screws began popping through the surface. How could it NOT have been infected is actually a more appropriate question.
4. I tightened it at 6:00 and 12:00 o'clock. That's right, the woman who had been unable to attend any doctor's appointments pretty much ever in the last ten years was now screwing her leg apart every six hours.
5. Note: Not really, but it hurt a lot.
6. http://www.medicinenet.com/reflex_sympathetic_dystrophy_syndrome/page2.htm

CHAPTER SEVENTEEN

A s my leg healed, my life with Phoebe went on. She was still half little girl, half angry, bitter woman. And she was growing up. She cared about fashion, music, and boys. She had an ocean of black wavy hair that I loved, and she started wearing make-up that I hated—dark, dramatic eyebrows, her beautiful full lips lined in black liner. She and her friends would go to the mall to a photo place called Star Shots[1] and get glamour pictures taken. Glamour pictures for which she and her friends never smiled because they didn't think smiling looked cool.

Phoebe had several friends in our neighborhood in Chula Vista. One of them had a handsome father. Not that I got my hopes up too high. I was a single mother, a felon, and—when this man and I first met—I still had the ilizarov on my leg from toe to knee—a huge, swollen, franken-leg. I wouldn't be auditioning as a runway model any time soon. Even so Miguel and I occasionally chatted. One day he came over to help me with my car. I'm not sure how he saw through the leg brace and stitches, but he must have seen some potential because we started dating soon thereafter.

Falling in love is complicated. But when he's going through a divorce and bringing two kids with their own baggage to the relationship, and you're bringing your own past, a criminal record, plus a child and all her baggage to the relationship, things can get really complicated really quickly.

Shortly before Miguel moved in, one of his girls wound up pregnant. Trying desperately to keep his daughter close and out of more trouble, Miguel invited his daughter and her boyfriend to live with us.

I had loved Miguel partly for his generosity. Now it just seemed like he couldn't say no to people. We argued about this constantly. We couldn't agree on how to parent, especially in regard to each other's children. That type of disagreement would have been hard no matter what. But as the years went on, it was even harder when Phoebe saw that I was parenting her with more strictness than her step-sister was getting. Why should she be punished for staying out all night when Carrie did? Why should she not be allowed to drive because she got caught at a party when Carrie had done the exact same thing and only gotten a 15-minute lecture? Why should she not be allowed to smoke in the house when Carrie did?

I didn't have good answers to those questions. *Because Carrie wasn't my daughter. Because I didn't have the final say on her life.* What ended up happening was a much lower standard for Phoebe than I would have liked, while she still felt she was being singled out and getting the short end of the stick in our mismatched parenting. Lose lose.

And yet, without my drug crutch for me to fall back on, for me to put above everything and everybody else, we managed to work through things. There were a lot of challenges, but there was also a lot of love. Miguel and I still didn't get married. Not only would marriage be a long-term emotional commitment, but it would create a financial loss as well.

At this point, my largest monetary contributions to our relationship were my social security and the Medicaid insurance for me and Phoebe. I was still dealing with the aftermath of my leg surgery, as well as depression and anxiety. Phoebe and I used a variety of expensive medications. If Miguel and I got married, I would lose at least eleven hundred dollars a month plus my insurance. And we really needed the money. Miguel worked as a welder. Although he worked hard, he still didn't earn a lot. Additionally, he sent several hundred dollars to his ex-wife for child support.[2] If I married him and lost my checks and insurance, I would land him with even more financial stress, and that didn't feel like the right thing to do to the man I loved.

At Randy's encouragement, Miguel got into the Boiler Makers Union. This brought him decent paying work. But we still lacked any significant job security. I couldn't do any regular work with my leg, but I babysat on the side and did my best to be a mother to two challenging teenage girls[3]. We lived in this limbo for a while, trying to figure ourselves out.

Which wasn't easy. I had left all ties to the drug world behind me—even the people like Matt and Trisha, whom I'd considered true friends. There were a few other friends I had promised I would always be there for, no matter what. One of these friends—a guy named Bill who used to buy meth from me and sell it—was now in jail. I had been writing to him, trying to encourage him. At one point, I'd even written that when he got out, we should go to lunch together.

When Miguel found the letter, he wasn't happy. He told me, "You're going to have to decide if you want to stay friends with these people from the drug world or stay with me."

At the time, this seemed really anal and uptight. After all, I was just trying to support people. I was just trying to keep the promises I'd made to them. But at Miguel's insistence I gave in and cut off my ties.

From that point on, I maintained absolutely no contact with any of my former friends or ties to my former life. To make the break even more complete, we moved to Las Vegas. Miguel worked as a boiler maker there and when he had dead time he would fly to Indiana where Randy was living and working, and do work there.

While in Vegas my father called with some bad news. He had been diagnosed with multiple myeloma—cancer of the bone and blood. My father and I had hit a few rocks in our lives, but we'd maintained a very close relationship. On the phone he told me that he wanted to walk his daughter down the aisle before he died.

What could I do? Miguel and I were married in August of 2002[4].

Shortly after, Randy told us we should move to Indiana. Miguel had been flying out there pretty regularly anyway, and Randy told him that if he went back to school for a bit, Randy could get him a job as a quality control inspector. So we moved. Miguel took some classes and got on at my brother's company. On top of that, when my father passed away, he left us a chunk of money with the instructions to use it to buy a house. I think he was worried we would waste it. We didn't. We put up a down payment for a house in a nice Midwestern neighborhood.

Now with a spanking new job and a pretty new house, we were actually making money—real money. After years of scrimping and saving, we had more money than we even knew what to do with. Guess what? We still had problems. Some of them shockingly large.

1. Yes, that was its real name.
2. I'm not saying that he shouldn't have, only that it meant more money out.
3. Phoebe and Carrie lived with us. Annie, Miguel's youngest daughter still lived with her mother at this point.
4. Make no mistake. Miguel and I had wanted to marry, but money and life had gotten in the way. My dad's request was the final nudge that pushed us to the altar.

PART III
INDIANA

CHAPTER EIGHTEEN

P hoebe had stayed in Nevada to go to Job Corps and complete her education there.[1] Her best friend had convinced her to do it and then her best friend had backed out. Phoebe still began at Job Corps, but she didn't stay long. After that she moved to Texas to stay with Carrie who had just gotten out of the service. And soon enough, Phoebe was in Indiana with us, but not happy about that either. She didn't know what she wanted or needed to do. I thought she should do Job Corps in Indiana (which she eventually did), but before she got to that point, she got her own apartment, and worked here and there and got a boyfriend here and there, and felt unhappy.

On top of that, Miguel's job, which had started in Evansville, now transferred him to a town three hours north of us. He would stay up there in a corporate apartment throughout the week and then come home on the weekends.

It was stressful to have my husband gone so much and my daughter drifting. It was the type of thing that often throws addicts back to their old habits. But at this point, the years had flown on. I was in my mid-forties. Phoebe was an adult;

I'd been with Miguel for ten years. I had been away from drugs for a long time—about twelve years, and I was 2000 miles away from the drug crowd I'd known.

Which isn't to say that I had developed any magical coping skills.

And so, without drugs, I turned to any other substances I could find to use as a bandage when I felt scraped up. I drank any time there was a problem of any level. I smoked like a steam engine. When I wasn't smoking and drinking, I had a shot (or four)[2] of espresso or drank Diet Coke.[3] At this point, I never thought, "I need to get high." But I often thought, "I need a pack of cigarettes.[4] Or a few shots of vodka. Or both."

I never drank beer or wine or any type of alcohol that might have been considered light weight. When I drank, I went for hard liquors like tequila and vodka,[5] which I often mixed into a diet soda. Then I could act like it *was* diet soda.

But I didn't worry about drinking. Drinking was legal. Alcohol could be purchased anywhere. This exonerated it from any worry for me. I'd been addicted to cocaine and meth. I'd tried heroin, and before I was pregnant, I'd used Quaaludes all the time in order to get really really wasted. Once I even did acid when my neighbors gave me a little purple pill and told me it was a diet pill. It wasn't. I was supposed to go with a friend to a Chinese wedding reception that night and, as I was putting on my make-up, it seemed like the lights started flashing. When I drove, I couldn't tell what color the street lights were. At the wedding reception, I kept looking at my hands, convinced they were covered in mud. I would wipe them off and the mud would still be there. Like a high little Lady Macbeth surrounded by Asian people at a wedding. So, yes, alcohol hardly seemed like a big deal.

Besides, it wasn't like I drank a lot. I mean, when I'd been on drugs, I'd drunk a *lot*. While on meth, I'd drunk heavily every single night.[6] Now I didn't. Which felt like a step up; and it was. Now I only drank about once a week. But when I did drink, I drank to escape, to run from myself through a couple of shots of tequila or a quick dose of vodka. If ever any issues arose in my life, I opened the liquor cabinet and let myself in. I tried to always have alcohol in the house, but when I didn't, I went over to my neighbor's house to get some. If I needed a shot, she'd hook me up; and if she needed a cup of sugar, I'd hook her up.

This was how I dealt with problems. And there were *a lot* of problems. Miguel's oldest was struggling now that she wasn't in the military. Soon enough, she was with lots of different men, eventually having babies with those different men, drinking way more than I did and getting involved with drugs herself[7], which broke my heart. Phoebe was trying to get her GED and find a decent job (and a decent man) and struggling intermittently with her health.

So was I. With my leg in a state of continual pain and swelling, I was being juggled through all types of medication. For several years after my surgery, I'd been too afraid to take any medicine at all. I had lived in a state of constant, intense pain. Then a doctor in Las Vegas had asked me why I forced myself to live like that. I didn't tell her about my drug past, but I did say that I was worried about being dependent on the pain meds. She said, "Oh, don't worry; we've got something new; and better. It's a long-acting pain medication and you only have to take it every twelve hours." Well, that did sound better—this magical new drug. Turns out it was OxyContin.[8]

In Indiana, my doctor was not impressed with this medication. He called it Hillbilly Heroin[9] and said to me, "You ready to try something new?" Well, I knew I didn't want Hillbilly Heroin, so, yes, I was ready to try something else. He prescribed me a new medicine called Fentanyl.

Fentanyl was supposed to be great and totally not dangerous and you could even use it as a patch. That sounded wonderful. Then I wouldn't have to think about it; and patches always made it feel like you weren't *taking* anything. Except those Fentanyl patches were forty times stronger than morphine, and up to fifty times more potent than heroine.

Even doctors didn't seem to fully understand what that meant at the time. But lately Fentanyl patches have been in the news because people have died from using them. I once saw a TV program where people were cutting the patches into tiny pieces. They would put them on their bodies to keep from going into withdrawal when they were visiting relatives and couldn't get heroin. Did you catch that? These patches— even pieces of these patches—were so potent that they could help addicts hide their addiction, keep them from going into withdrawal. Not only that, but there are now plenty of people not trying to hide anything, and just straight up abusing the patches. This is called "smoking the patch." You heard me. People will put the patch on tin foil, heat it till it smokes, and then inhale the smoke.

But at the time, I didn't know any of this (and neither did my doctor). I took my pain meds like a good girl, and I usually felt less pain. But over time, I gave up on the idea of ever being able to live med free, not because I felt addicted to the medicine (miraculously), but because the pain in my leg was still so intense that I couldn't imagine dealing with it for the rest of my life.

But guess what? Pain and pain medications aren't exactly great for relationships.

With all these problems and so few actual coping skills, Phoebe and I would drag each other into the nastiest fights. When she came to my house, it was often with a chip on her shoulder. She'd walk through the door, and I'd see her face and think, "Oh boy, here it comes." And it did. She'd rip into me with something completely unreasonable. Maybe she had asked me to do something and she didn't think I'd done it. Or maybe she'd dig into our past. "If you loved me, you never would have let me get molested." And my heart would break into a million pieces. But you wouldn't know that because I'd cuss and then scream back, "I don't even know why I worked so hard to get you back. You don't even want me."

Eventually it seemed we could do almost nothing together without it turning into a huge issue. I used to drive to her house in order to bring her groceries or give her rides when she didn't have a car. I would call beforehand to tell her I'd be there in five minutes. And, inevitably, I'd get there and she wouldn't be at all ready to leave. That would start it. I'd be standing there waiting, my leg in pain, on fire. And I'd get so angry, thinking about how she didn't even care. As soon as she came out, I'd rip into her. "I told you I was going to be here in five minutes. I don't understand why you can't be ready." She'd respond with something snarky and we were off.

It got to the point where if we were in the car and we were arguing, I would have to pull over because otherwise, Phoebe would open the door and jump out, no matter how fast we were going. If she couldn't jump out of cars, she would sometimes hit things. Once she broke a window in the house, slicing up her arm. Any word either of us said—no matter how small the issue, no matter how small the irritation or problem—would turn into a full-on, blow-out fight.

Eventually, Miguel's youngest daughter, Annie, moved into our house with us. She was fifteen or so at the time, and she got caught in the middle of it all—forced to walk through a field of landmines. Annie used to say to me, "Mom, we need to go to a church." Which was odd because nobody I knew went to church[10]. I didn't even believe in God at this point. But still she would say it, out of the blue. "Mom we need to go to church."

When Miguel was home, I tried my best to shield him from all the crazy that was going on. He had a kidney issue, which affected his cholesterol and blood pressure. It would become aggravated through stress. My solution was to hide any stress from him. The problem was that there was just so much stress from all of our children. Not only that, but when I was bugged by the things Miguel did, I would hold them in, thinking this was better. Except that then I'd get drunk and blow out every awful thing that had been on my mind or bothering me. The next day things were always a disaster. And soon enough, he'd be away again—back at work and out of town. As he progressed in his career, he started travelling even more.

This left me with the girls.[11] It left me with his oldest and her babies. It left me with Phoebe and her depression and her carpal tunnel and her diabetes and the men who would come live with her, sitting on their butts while she went to work. It left me with Annie—the last teenager living at home.

The truth was that when Annie and I were alone, we lived in a state of relative peace. With her dad working out of town and her sisters out of the house, I was finally able to tighten the parenting reins. When Annie was sixteen, Miguel and I bought her a car—a sporty green Grand Am that she loved. I told her that she, and only she, was allowed to drive this car. If she let anyone else drive it, I would not allow her to drive it for a full month. Within weeks, she'd gone out with a boy and let him drive the car. Away went the car. Each morning, she had to get up, walk past her new car, and take the school bus, which she hated. Each night Miguel called and asked when I was going to give her the car again. *When thirty days was up, that's when*. Which was the right choice. Which was the type of parenting that—years later—gets you a phone call from that child thanking you for being strict, for teaching her to keep her word and follow through. But it's also the type of parenting that is very hard in the moment. I wasn't used to dealing with things that were hard in the moment. I was learning, but there was a steep curve.

THE FACT THAT I GOT ALONG WITH ANNIE DIDN'T EXACTLY help Phoebe (even though she got along with Annie too). Phoebe used to accuse me of treating the other girls better than I treated her. Which wasn't true. Miguel's daughters weren't yelling at me all the time. If they had been, they wouldn't have gotten the pass Phoebe got. When all was said and done, I loved Phoebe with my all and everything. There was nothing she could say or do to me that would change that. In a lot of ways Phoebe had something no one else in my life did—she could scream all she wanted and I would still love her the next day.

And she would love me too—even though I jumped on her back a lot of the time when she came over, even though I was in automatic defense mode before she even opened her mouth. Even though Miguel used to say, "Why do you need to talk to her like that? She hasn't done anything yet." Even though, after she did do something—because she always did —Annie would say, "Please, Mom, just don't respond." Even though I would respond, and not kindly. Even though the two of us kept doing things we knew we shouldn't, things we didn't even necessarily want to do. Even though even though even though. Through it all we still loved each other.

We just didn't know how to do it right.

1. With Job Corps, you get your GED, live on a little campus, and learn a skill that you can use to get a job.
2. Yes, I would drink four shots of espresso at a time. When I bought an espresso maker for my house, I always made the largest amount possible, and then drank it right up.
3. I used to buy cases of Diet Coke and drink them one after another until they were all gone.
4. Virginia Slims Menthols, if you please. I'd been smoking these ever since I was a girl. I'd seen a commercial with a young, beautiful woman walking along a beach with a hot guy. Virginia Slims got thirty years of business from me for that ad.
5. Which, supposedly, cannot be smelled on your breath.
6. Cocaine and meth users do this—drink alcohol to bring them down from the intense highs.
7. I wash my hands from that, though. There was absolutely no drug influence brought into her life through me.
8. You know, the highly addictive drug that's leading tons of teens and pain patients into a life of opiate addiction—sometimes turning them to the streets to get the fix they now need.
9. And it's gotten to the point now that you could call it suburban-whoever heroin because its abuse is a very pervasive problem.
10. Except Randy who didn't count because he was always a goody goody two shoes.
11. The oldest two didn't live in the house, but they did live in the area.

CHAPTER NINETEEN

At this point, Phoebe was still having violent mood swings, had started drinking herself, and would also use pot regularly. She told me it was the only way to take the edge off, mellow out, feel happy. But the effects of this mellowing never lasted. The next day she was always extra uptight, angry, and depressed. I told her drugs could ruin her life, or at the very least that they would disrupt her in all the worst ways. I told her that there were other ways to deal with problems or moods or setbacks. Constant lectures she didn't want to hear. Constant lectures she didn't believe. Because how could I say there were other ways to deal with problems when I could barely cope myself. And so I told her the one thing I knew for sure: "You're gonna get caught."

And then one day she did. She had some weed packaged up to sell at Job Corps. She got pulled over. And there we were with history repeating itself. It hurt. It hurt that I couldn't help her even with that one simple thing, couldn't keep her from making the same stupid mistakes I had.

Getting caught doesn't always help. But sometimes it does. Eventually it had for me. And Phoebe proved to be a quicker learner. I got her a lawyer and she agreed to take drug classes so that she could get her record changed from a felony to a misdemeanor. Afterwards, she was on probation. It was a tune I knew too well, a story that was uncomfortably familiar. But when I started getting stressed, when I started to sink, Phoebe would say, "Don't worry, Mom; I'm going to doper class." It's not really the thing you aspire to hear from your child, but the truth is that at that point in our relationship, it was a heck of a lot better than most of the alternatives.

And so Phoebe went to doper class and I continued to drink away my problems and smoke away my stress. Carrie had moved to an apartment and was expecting her fourth baby from her fourth man. Miguel was in Terre Haute dealing with his own stress in his own negative ways—ways that would haunt us later. The only mildly sane one among us was Annie—caught in the middle of all these opposing forces, like we were a family of magnets, trying to connect, and instead banging off of each other as though the wrong poles had been jammed together.

We were all a whole lot of hot mess. With my marriage quickly descending into flaming status. In the last weeks and months, I had started to feel as though there was a distance with Miguel—a distance bigger than the physical miles that separated us. He was often away for work, usually for a week at a time. Each time we talked on the phone, he felt like someone else, aloof and distracted; and when he came home on the weekends, he always seemed closed and unavailable. It was easy to excuse it away—who *would* want to be fully there when our kids were a disaster and we were barely hanging on? But time and distance were eating us up as time and distance had eaten up thousands of couples before us. And it wasn't good.

About a year and a half after Miguel began travelling for

work, I got a phone call. It was a woman, seven months pregnant, who believed Miguel to be the father. She believed it with good cause. They'd been dating for over a year and then he'd stopped contacting her.

I lost my mind. To the sadness. To the anger. To the betrayal and shock. I called Phoebe and Annie, and said, "Bring me two packs of cigarettes and a bottle of Tanqueray. Now." They did. I paced back and forth in the living room all night, drinking, smoking, and crying. I didn't sleep. I didn't eat. My girls worried over me. The next day, they took me to the emergency room for a psychiatric evaluation, not sure what else to do, how to keep me safe when I was so low.

CHAPTER TWENTY

In the midst of all this, my nephew—Randy's oldest son—
had come home from his Mormon mission[1], gotten
married, finished school, gotten a job, and had a baby. Randy
had tried to convince me to come to church for decades. He'd
tried so long and so hard that he was done trying. In fact, he'd
tried so long and so hard that he had started discouraging
others from trying—worried that I would shove away from
them like I'd often shoved away from Randy when he'd
pushed too hard. "No," Randy had told his son when Danny
mentioned talking to me about church. "I've talked to her a
thousand times and she doesn't want it. We're not going to
force it on her."

One night when my nephew Danny was having dinner
with his family and a couple of Mormon[2] missionaries, they
asked him if there was anyone he thought would benefit from
their message. Well, he sure thought I could benefit from
something, but he wasn't sure if he should share my name.
He'd looked at his wife, and she had shrugged. "Yes," Danny
had said. "I need you to visit my aunt. Just ring the doorbell
and start talking."

So they did. But they didn't talk to me. If I had answered the door, I would have found these young missionary girls pleasant and naïve; and then I would have sweetly dismissed them. But I couldn't. My husband answered the door and when he did, they started talking to him in Spanish. That was fun for him. They chatted for at least twenty minutes and at the end of it, he'd made an appointment for them to come back.

"What!?" I asked when he finally came back inside.

"They were just so nice," he said.

"Whatever," I said. "Just know that I'm not going to take part in all that religious crazy."

And I didn't. I still couldn't understand how a God could let a child be molested, and I worried that if I started dabbling in religion, that would be a type of betrayal towards Phoebe. Even if I'd been interested in their message I wouldn't have wanted to hear it with my husband at this point. We were struggling.

On the day the missionaries were to come over for their visit, I got another phone call—this one from the doctor confirming that the paternity test was positive. Miguel was the father of another woman's child[3]. I had known it was coming, but that positive test was a final nail in a months' old coffin. I called my husband. We argued. I slammed down the phone.

He called back and told me to call the sister missionaries and cancel the appointment he'd set up. After all, he wasn't going to be able to make it. The appointment was in twenty minutes. "Whatever," I said. "That's so rude. They can come over. I'll just talk to them for a bit."

Two shots of vodka later, I opened the door and smiled at the two female missionaries. "Hi!" I said, all fake cheer. "He's not here, but you can talk to me." And they did. For two and a half hours while I cried about problems in my life and marriage that I didn't feel I could tell them.

At their next visit, I said, "I'm an atheist, but you guys can come and see me. You can be my Mormon therapists."

Before they left, they stood on the doorstep and asked, "Do you mind if we pray for you?"

Right there, on the welcome mat? Yeah, whatever. I'm sure they weren't the first (and they wouldn't be the last) people in this world who had prayed for me. I truly wasn't even interested in listening to their prayer. But as they prayed for me I felt a feeling go through me—like a whoosh of air, a door opening on a breezy day. It felt light. It felt good. It was different than anything I had ever felt before. All the next week I felt calm. All the next week I could handle the array of problems that continually insisted on stomping through my life.

When Phoebe and Annie talked to me on the phone, they were expecting my normal wrecked self, but instead I said, "Whatever's going to happen is going to happen. I don't have any control over it." I'm sure they spent the rest of the day looking under the beds for their real mother—the depressed, sometimes drunk one. But she was nowhere to be found.

I still didn't go to church. I let the sister missionaries come over and give me the lessons, but still considered myself an atheist. I would say, "I don't believe in God. I'll never believe in God. But you can come." I didn't know how to believe in God. How could I believe in someone who had let such horrible things happen to me, who had let such horrible things happen to my daughter?

Still, the sisters came. They'd teach a lesson or offer to clean my house. It was so foreign to me, how helpful they were with no expectation of anything in return. It was completely different from all of the people I'd known in the life I'd lived before, even in the life I was living now.

My nephew, Danny, was different too. He and his wife were obviously in love, mutually caring for their baby who had been born eight weeks too early, supporting each other through the stress of that situation and helping each other out as they worked through the early stages of their careers and the care of their family.[4] Whenever you went to Danny's house, you could feel the quiet, you could almost touch the soft sense of peace. And Danny wasn't about to give up on his jaded old aunt.

The first time I went to church was because my great-niece was getting a baby's blessing. Danny invited me to come, and my brother wanted me there. So, fine, I would go to church.

No one really expected me to stay past the first meeting. My brother Randy was ready to take me home after the first hour. "We can go," he said.

"No, it's okay. We can stay," I replied. Three hours of church. That's what Mormons did. I stayed the whole time—through the main meeting and the adult Sunday school lesson and the women's meeting.

My nephew Danny asked me how I liked it. "It was cool," I said.

He invited me to come back.

"No, that's okay," I said.

Everyone had been really nice to me. People talked to me, asked questions, included me in the services. That didn't mean I fit in. That didn't mean I belonged in a church. I knew I was different. I knew that, at this point, I looked like a normal middle-class housewife. But I knew that I'd lived a life of drugs and crime, a life that most people in the congregation couldn't even begin to imagine. I knew my family life was nothing like theirs.

For several months I didn't go back. But the missionaries kept coming. They kept inviting me—challenging me—to go to church. Eventually, I said okay. I've broken some promises in my life, but the truth is that—drug addict or not—I've never liked it. Consequently, at 11:00 am when the services started, I was sitting in a pew by Danny. The same thing happened the next time I went. And the next.

The mornings before I went were always hard. I was on pain medication that made me extremely hot and it was hard to find things to wear when I just wanted to hang out in a t-shirt and shorts all day. Sometimes I'd sit in church wanting a cigarette or an espresso. Yet every time I went to church I got to see my great-niece. That was pretty good motivation. She would come up to me, wanting to sit on my lap and say, "Hi Aunt Lolla." Seeing the way my nephew and his wife raised their child was striking. I also started to notice that when I went to church, the days afterwards passed more peacefully and my week was always better. It was an odd change, a subtle one that I hadn't been looking for or expecting.

In my life I had gotten used to big changes, to fireworks and the ensuing fires. Now, even when it didn't seem like anything was happening, tiny things were. In my own heart, but also in my family.

One of the reasons I'd been worried about going to church was that I knew it might hurt Phoebe—attending a church after all we'd been through, when the man who'd hurt her had been a faithful church-goer. It felt disloyal to her, and the more involved I became, the more I worried it would hurt her feelings. Until one day, out of the blue, she said, "Hey Mom. If it's good for you, go do it." And it did seem to be good for me, so I continued to go do it.

IF YOU KNOW ANYTHING ABOUT MEMBERS OF THE CHURCH OF Jesus Christ of Latter-day Saints, you know that they do more than go to church. They don't smoke; they don't drink alcohol or coffee. In fact, they pretty much don't do any of the things I was used to doing to stay sane. Additionally, they work for free in clergy-type jobs that other churches pay people to do. They visit and serve one another. They fast once a month. They pray and read the Bible and other scriptures on a regular basis.

I didn't know how I felt about any of those things. I didn't even know how to pray. In fact, the missionaries had to give me a card (I still have it) with instructions on how to pray. Even with my card, I wasn't sure I could pray to a God I didn't believe in. It seemed hypocritical, so I would pray, "To God if there is a God."

That's how I started.

The very smallest step of the very smallest faith. But as I took it, small blessings started popping into my life. These blessings weren't phenomenal; they weren't what anyone would call miraculous, but they were also not normal for my life, and I couldn't ignore them.

In the scriptures, God challenges us to experiment upon the word. I didn't know anything about that yet, but as I noticed small, good things coming into my large, wrecked life, my heart began to give way a little bit, to make the smallest spot for a God if He happened to want to come in and stay a while.

At first I wasn't praying regularly, or probably correctly. And then, bit by bit, I kind of was. I couldn't kneel with my leg, so I would pray in my bed or car or sitting on the couch. Every day.

Reading, however, was a different matter. I barely even read my email, much less fat books of scripture, written in archaic English. I hated reading and couldn't focus, especially on the scriptures with all the *thee*'s and *thou*'s and *it came to passes*. As a result, the missionaries would bring over videos for me to watch. That was feel-good enough for me, but the missionaries would still challenge me every week to read from the scriptures.

I felt terrible telling them I would and then not doing it over and over, so one week, right before they arrived, I pulled out the copy of the *Book of Mormon* they'd given me, opened it up, closed my eyes, and randomly pointed at a verse. That scripture[5] said that I should make a recording of my own life[6]. And that one tiny scripture made me feel something, made me realize that maybe the story of my life would and could help someone—God's spirit moving into my mind, even through the small, crooked efforts I was making.

Reading consistently was still a struggle for me, although in time, I began to read the church magazines and other bits of scriptures.[7]

I kept doing these little things until, one day, I quit smoking.

Okay, it wasn't quite that easy.

I had smoked since I was twelve. Of all the habits I'd ever had (and if you've gotten this far in this book, you know I had some *habits*), smoking was the hardest to give up. I had tried nicotine gum, herbal supplements, nicotine patches, just about everything. None of it had worked. My brother Randy used to say that I might as well roll up the patch and smoke it. It was kind of true. In fact, sometimes when I was wearing a nicotine patch, I would still smoke a cigarette. The nicotine overdose would make me sick to my stomach, but I still wanted, still felt I needed that cigarette. I didn't love them; in fact, at this point, I hated them, but I craved them. If I didn't get one, it affected me physically. Without them, I felt like I'd been kicked in the gut.

My husband didn't smoke, and he didn't like my smoking. That meant that whenever I smoked, I'd go outside. And it meant that every time I was in my car, I smoked. Soon enough, being in my car or outside made me want to smoke.

No matter where I was, if I ran out of cigarettes, I would *have* to go get some—even if it was inconvenient, even if it would make me late to something, even if I was just sitting at home in my pajamas with no other reason to leave the house.

One of these times—when I made a quick trip to the gas station to buy another pack of cigarettes—I started complaining to the sales girl about my habit. "I hate that it has this kind of control over me. I mean, I *have* to leave the house to get it."

The girl was young and blond. She got my cigarettes, then looked at me and said, "Why don't you buy one of those Nicotrol inhalers? My grandpa smoked for years. He quit with the inhalers. So did my aunt."

I called my doctor the next day and he wrote me a prescription.

No one really thought they would work. I'd already tried to quit a bunch of times with a bunch of methods. And the inhaler didn't look extremely impressive. It was a white plastic tube that you'd stick a nicotine pellet in and then you'd inhale. It was like a white, plastic cigar. Or, as my brother Randy put it, "How long you going to suck on that thing? It looks like a tampon."[8]

That inhaler, however, was incredibly effective at removing my cravings. And then, one day, I noticed that I hadn't even used the inhaler for a few days. Soon enough I didn't need it or cigarettes anymore.

Those cigarettes were the last tie to any drinking I might have been tempted to do. I had already mostly quit drinking. Now with the cigarettes completely gone, there was no other trigger or association, and the drinking went away completely.

At this point, I had gone to church on and off for two years. I'll admit that in those first few months, I went mostly out of loyalty to the sweet little missionaries who had listened to more of my problems than they had probably cared to hear. And to see Danny's family and sit with my great-nieces, which was a perfect little bribe.

Over time, however, I noticed that the people there were always happy. It sounds cliché, doesn't it, maybe even boring. But it was the truth. In my normal life, I wasn't around people who were happy. At the church, I was. Those happy people were always trying to make me feel included and loved and also happy. It made an impact. I used to ask the missionaries why they were so happy, and they would say, "It's the gospel."

It was an answer that never satisfied me. It seemed too easy, too naïve, too right-there-in-my-face to be true. So I would think to myself, "Nah, it's got to be something else."

Still, I must not have had myself completely convinced because by the end of those two years, I had quit most of the stuff I was supposed to quit and started doing most of the stuff I was supposed to do. People weren't pressuring me to do any of it. In fact, if anything, people were trying really hard to *not* pressure me.

One night, I went to Danny's house to have dinner, and he asked me, "What's keeping you from getting baptized?"

The floodgates opened and I told him everything about what had happened to Phoebe, and how I couldn't join the church because it still seemed that on some level God had betrayed her. Danny had lots of answers. He asked a lot of questions too, including whether I could forgive William Tong (I couldn't). And then he said lots of perfectly rational, reasonable things, none of which filled the hole in me that couldn't be filled.

But Diana—a mother herself—quietly and maybe a little fiercely quoted a passage of scripture. "Offences will come: but woe unto him, through whom they come! It were better for him that a millstone were hanged about his neck, and he cast into the sea, than that he should offend one of these little ones."[9] I had never heard this scripture before, and it was exactly how I felt. For the first time it seemed that maybe God and I were on the same team, that we both considered certain things unacceptable, that He understood me.

Something freed in my heart.

A few months later, I brought Danny some soup I'd made for him and his family. He came to get the heavy pot from my car and then, out of nowhere, I said, "I think I'll get baptized." No one had even asked me the question.

If Danny had a tiny heart attack when he heard it, he didn't show it. Instead, he celebrated, calling people like my brother Randy, and our friends Ed and Sally. There were no fireworks, but I knew that this church was pulling my life in the right direction. And it was about time.

Later Randy called me back, almost as though trying to scare me away from the church. I think that after all those years watching me destroy myself he was afraid that I didn't understand that this wasn't just some quick fix, some high. This was a commitment, and I would need to work to keep my faith. Later when I talked to Danny about it, he said, "Don't worry, Aunt Laura. Dad hasn't seen the changes in you; we have."

And there were many changes. I had stopped smoking

and drinking. To be honest, that made everyone happy. But the biggest change was one that was harder to see. I had stopped cussing and screaming so much. My house was quieter, more peaceful. I guess that's because the things going on inside of me were quieter and more peaceful, too. And at first that little point inside of me was where it stopped. Everything else around me rolled on like it always had. People would come home and start arguing and swearing, slamming doors, stomping into bedrooms.

But I wouldn't. And then, like a stone dropped into the water, the ripples somehow started to swim across the pond. Within a few months, everybody was cussing and screaming less. In certain ways, this was my first experience with grace. I had made a change, a simple change. I had expected that change to affect me and me alone. And that was good enough. But somehow, shockingly, this change had started to extend, to grow—the flicker of a match catching onto bits of wood at first and then rising into a warm, bright flame.

Now, instead of bracing myself for a fight when Phoebe crossed the threshold, I prepared myself not to fight. Sometimes Phoebe would still bait me, sitting on the porch and swearing while she talked to her friends on the phone, or saying things like, "I'm so screwed up and it's your fault." But instead of biting back, I stopped taking the bait. We'd been stuck in an intense game of tug-of-war—both of us holding tight to our rope, leaning back, digging in our heels—determined to pull until the other person fell and got dragged over the loser line.

Then, all the sudden I put down my end. Phoebe held hers a tiny bit longer—wondering what to do with it when it was so slack, wondering if she could get me to somehow pick it up again. And then all the sudden she dropped her end, too.

People think of miracles as large, life-altering events—the

blind are healed or the dead are raised. One of the miracles I remember most was when one of my kids cussed in our house and then looked at me and said, "Oh, sorry Mom."

THAT SAID, SOMETIMES THE LAME ARE HEALED AS WELL, OR at least they get well enough to go to Walmart without having to limp and slouch against the wall.

Even though I had quit smoking and drinking, I still had significant struggles with my health. My leg was a constant battle—always inflamed and swollen. I was also on anti-depressants, taking all kinds of medicines for all kinds of problems.

The anti-depressants went first. I just didn't feel like I needed them anymore. I told my doctor that I'd found Christ, and didn't feel depressed. In fact, I told him I was so happy I might explode if I took an anti-depressant. I'm pretty sure he expected to see me back in his office in a couple of weeks begging for more. And I won't say that I haven't ever been depressed or low since, but the need for the drug went away, and didn't come back.

Then my bishop challenged me to give up the coffee for real (I'd kind of given it up several times, but kept returning to it). I pushed back a little. Coffee wasn't that big of a deal. *Everyone* drank coffee.

And it was just so hard to give up. While I'm being a little too honest, let me say that I couldn't even poop without coffee.[10] I'd been in the habit of going to Starbucks several times a day. I would always go with my dog and order an espresso mud coffee—super strong. My dog Nikki always got a treat too—her little pup cup with a tiny whirl of whipped cream and a dog biscuit buried inside it.[11]

The good people of Starbucks weren't idiots. Soon

enough, every time I drove past the Starbucks with Nikki in the car, she'd start to go nuts, panting, turning circles, whining. My baby wanted her pup cup.[12] I felt sorry for the poor little thing[13] so even when I was trying to quit drinking coffee, I would pull in. Just for a pup cup. But I'd pull out with more than that.

I told my bishop all of these very good reasons I had to have coffee[14]. I told him it helped me. I told him how hard it was to give it up.

He looked over his desk at me with a face that said, *Really Laura*. And then he said, "After everything else you've quit, are you really going to let coffee get you in the end."[15]

Fine, whatever, I guess I had technically been addicted to crystal meth and cocaine, not to mention my dependence on alcohol, cigarettes, and anti-depressants. "When do you want me to quit?" I said.

"Today," he replied like there was no other answer in the world.

WITHIN DAYS OF QUITTING, THE INFLAMMATION IN MY LEG had gone down, along with a good deal of the pain—pain that had been so crippling that there had been times when I had gone to run errands and had found myself hobbling through the store in so much agony I could barely see the people I passed, days when I couldn't go out at all, days when my nerves were on fire. If I sat down for fifteen to thirty minutes and then stood up, it felt like I was walking on broken glass. I couldn't put any weight on my foot at all until I'd gotten it working first. It was always swollen to at least a third bigger than its regular size, sometimes double. And it was always inflamed, red, and hot.

And then, within a few weeks, it wasn't.

Now we were into the realm of real honest to goodness miracles where those who are crippled can suddenly walk. The miracle hadn't come from the touch of God's hand, but from a simple obedience to what I was coming to believe were God's words.

All my life, I'd been kicking against the rules. All my life, I'd been wondering where this God was and why he was leaving me to drag through the sludge on my own. All my life I'd looked at those people "chained" by their religions and wondered why they would let a bunch of starched old folks tell them what to do. All my life, I'd been missing it, swatting away the hands that stretched out to pull me up, kicking away the God who would have helped me if I'd so much as looked in His direction.

I knew I'd never be as perfect as some of my church friends seemed to be. I knew I could never unmake the decisions I'd already made with my life. Yet, somehow God could unravel some of the tragedy that had come along with those choices. At a certain point I realized that I would do the best I could do for myself. It was a bright open window in my new life.

This is a lot of God talk all of the sudden. I know. I'm as surprised about it as you are. Maybe more so. But that's how it was. I hated God for a good part of my life. Then I simply gave up on believing in Him at all. Then, all the sudden, there He was and we were kind of hanging out together.

---

1. Many young adults from the Church of Jesus Christ of Latter-day Saints serve an 18-24 month mission away from home.
2. Members of the Church of Jesus Christ of Latter-day Saints are trying to move away from the nickname "Mormon," but at the time, that was

the only term I knew for them. Consequently, throughout this book, I'll use the nickname as I would have used it at the time.

3. This hurt extra hard because prior to that Miguel and I had been trying to have a child, but had been unsuccessful. On several levels. First, we had struggled to conceive. When we finally did conceive, we had struggled to produce a healthy baby, and we lost the baby at five months.

4. Diana primarily cared for the baby, though she worked as a nurse one day a week. Danny worked full time, but he was also actively involved in his family life.

5. 1 Nephi 1: 17, "But I shall make an account of my proceedings in my days…"

6. P.S. Here's that record; you're welcome.

7. It took me a few years, but now I can read, focus, and understand. The great thing about the whole process is that taking years was fine as long as I kept on with my tiny, baby steps.

8. Thanks, Randy. For the record, Randy is now always asking me the name of the inhaler so he can recommend it to his friends who are trying to quit.

9. Luke 17: 1-2 And, yes, she quoted it straight up from the King James Bible like that.

10. Yup. I had to use an herbal supplement when I did quit, until I got my body back to normal.

11. For the record, I was spending up to fifteen dollars at Starbucks a day —with my three coffees, tips, and coffee for my daughter or dog or whoever I was with. Later, after I'd stopped drinking coffee, I drew a little skull and crossbones on my Starbucks coffee cup. Then I wrote, "Save $1200/year—ask me how." Nobody has yet, but they really should.

12. Yes, yes, I did just tell you my dog was addicted to Starbucks.

13. Even though, truth be told, Starbucks wasn't good for Nikki either. The cream never sat well with her. Didn't mean she didn't want it. I hear you, Nikki, I do.

14. Except maybe the pooping and the pup cup, which must have been too embarrassing, but are somehow the only reasons I can really remember to write about in this memoir.

15. But the pup cup…

CHAPTER TWENTY-ONE

M iguel did not come to my baptism. He was out of the country—working at a new job that took him overseas where he would work on a project for a few years and then they'd move him to a different country—China, Saudi Arabia, Mongolia.

The day I got baptized was New Year's Day 2012. Right after my baptism, my friend (and Sunday school teacher) told me, "Don't think your challenges are over. Satan doesn't like what just happened. He'll be after you harder than ever now."

I replied, "Are you kidding? I'm a stubborn Irish girl. Once my mind is made up, nothing can change it."

Besides, I was sure Satan would give me a break for a couple hours, right?[1]

That afternoon, Miguel called and asked, "What'd you do today?"

"Well, I got baptized."

Not the answer he expected. Later that day I would receive an email from my husband telling me, "You know, we're just going to drift further and further apart. You'll have all your friends there. We won't have anything in common."

He didn't say the word 'divorce' but it was all over that email, smeared between the lines. We had been through some serious crap. But I didn't want to get divorced. And I hadn't thought he wanted to get divorced either. The truth was that he didn't. But he was hurt—hurt that I had joined a strange church when I'd consistently refused to attend a Catholic mass with him, hurt that my intentions and heart were being drawn elsewhere. He didn't realize at the time that by having my heart, mind, and actions go first to God that there would be a lot of extra left over for him. He didn't realize that if we gave up our five measly loaves, we'd wind up with a whole bunch of bread.

I didn't really either. I wrote him back, and said, "I'm sorry you're so offended. If I'd known it was going to offend you so much, I wouldn't have done it, because you're my first priority." Then I went to my friend's house and cried.

I spent days in bed, depressed and mourning. Besides the fact that I didn't want to divorce, I also didn't know what I would do if Miguel left. I had no income, a gimpy leg, and a felony record. How would I care for myself? Who else would or could love a person like me? I was a complete disaster as I was every time something went a little wrong with Miguel.

The days ticked forward. As far as I can remember my husband didn't respond to my email. We moved forward in a sort of uncomfortable silence. He didn't ask. I didn't tell. Under the unspoken terms of this strange and slightly dysfunctional truce, I still went to church, but each week during church I would go outside and call him overseas at our usual time. I never talked about going to church or said anything more about it. I'm not sure if he knew I was still going or not. I'm not sure what he thought at all. But when he came home, he saw the change in me.

Seeing your husband only once every three months isn't

usually the best thing for a marriage, but at this point in our lives, it worked to my favor. Miguel came home to a calmer, happier person than he had left, a person who was in less pain, a person who could get along with her daughter. I was more put together mentally and emotionally than Miguel had ever seen me. It was like the before and after pictures for a diet pill. You might not notice the changes very much when you're seeing them day by day, but when a big chunk of time has elapsed and you see that person again, all the sudden you're like, "Whoa."

Miguel was like, "Whoa." After that I kept going to church with his somewhat blessing. Then, every three months when I would see him, I had changed some more.

At first, each time before he came home, I'd asked for a blessing[2] from two of my church teachers. I asked so regularly that I started to feel like some kind of blessing stalker. The truth was that the blessings were working so well that I felt almost afraid not to get one. It took me a while to realize that there wasn't some kind of magic juice in those blessings that was making my time with Miguel better. It was the fact that I was changing, that I was kinder and happier. Sure, the blessings were helping, mostly by giving me a boost of heavenly confidence. But in time, I found that even if I didn't get a blessing before Miguel came home, we got along and had a great time together.

In our old life together, I had been a little time bomb of attitude and anger. Now he came home to a loving, caring wife. I wasn't exactly making warm cookies and wandering around in aprons, but he and I were both pretty happy that there was nothing in the house that needed repair because it had gotten broken in a family fight.

Within the next few years, we would start taking trips together, travelling all over the world. Miguel no longer wanted or needed to escape from me. In fact, it seemed to me that he missed me pretty badly when he was gone, always wanting to meet up, to go on a couple's vacation, to spend as much time together as our busy lives would allow. We spent time in Thailand, Dubai, China, and Indonesia.

For many years, we were wonderfully, solidly happy.

Drug free, happy, and riding a camel!

At that point in our lives, Miguel never would have asked for his Before Mormon[3] wife back. She was a nut job.

THE TRUTH IS THAT NO ONE WAS BEGGING BEFORE MORMON Mom to come back either.

Phoebe and I started to spend more and more time together—going to the movies and lunch, enjoying each other's company. We would talk and laugh and—most importantly—we weren't *afraid* to be around each other. We weren't worried that if we spent two minutes together, something would blow. Before, that had always been how it felt —a simmering fear that any time we spent together would end in a crazy explosion. Now, it became easy to be together. More than easy—it was fun. And when we weren't together, we'd talk on the phone. Every day. It was something we wanted to do, something I missed if it didn't happen.

Phoebe had always had a giant heart, doing nice things for other people, trying to help them if they were going through tough times. Even in our roughest years, she would have dropped everything on earth if I'd needed her. And she often had. She'd been by my side when I was sick or struggling or broken-hearted.

Strangely, what we had the most trouble with in my pre-church life were the times when there wasn't a desperate need, the times that should have been *easy*. Those we filled with stress and argument, with ugly words and hurtful accusations.

Now we didn't. For the first time in a very long time, Phoebe and I were finding enjoyment in each other. We'd always had love—deep and hard and bold. As we slowly learned to trust each other, we found that we could keep that love while still allowing the edges to soften, while opening up the tough outer casing we'd used to protect ourselves, and letting the other person in.

I'd always given Phoebe a lot of stuff—ever since she was a baby. I hadn't known how to give her anything else. I'm not even sure I'd known what else there was to give. My life at that point hadn't had room for things like time and energy, thoughts and memories. Things that couldn't be quantified or held in one's hand. By the time I joined the church there were years of emotional debts just sitting there, waiting for me to figure out how to pay them.

I decided, at the advice of a friend, to make Phoebe a memory box for Christmas. I'd never done anything so sentimental before. I spent hours finding pictures of her, especially when she was little. I dug out an old Christmas ornament from the first Christmas we spent together after I was off drugs and I had custody. We'd had almost no money, so we'd gone to the dollar store to buy cheap bunches of fake flowers along with silver and gold spray paint (I told you I painted everything). We'd taken the flower bunches apart and then painted them silver and gold to hang on the tree. They are still my favorite ornaments, and I found one to put into her box.

To this I added movie tickets, gift cards. And then, an eighteen-page letter starting out with how happy I had been when I found out I was pregnant. I'd wanted that baby so badly. I'd been thrilled when, after forty hours of labor and a C-section, they'd taken her out and said, "It's a girl." Just like I had hoped.

And what a girl—so beautiful, so perfect. I'd played with and coddled her, worried myself to pieces when she was sick. All of these stories and pictures—many of them things Phoebe had never seen or heard—I put into her memory box. It was the first time I gave her something so wholly me, so completely *us*. And she loved it more than any of the expensive things I'd gotten her in all the years before.

---

1. Wrong.
2. Members of the Church of Jesus Christ of Latter-day Saints believe in the laying on of hands.
3. The woman I affectionately began to refer to as BM Laura.

CHAPTER TWENTY-TWO

A s I became involved with the church, I became less comfortable with one small, unresolved detail in my life. For the last thirty years, I'd been driving without a license. Way back when I'd first been dating Tim in Hawaii, I'd often felt depressed. Naturally, when I felt that way, I would get hammered. Twice, driving home, I got nailed with a DUI. They saddled me with a huge fine, which I never paid. Why should I? I could still drive just fine. And I did.

When I was in California dealing drugs, driving without a license hardly seemed like my biggest concern. In fact, if you'd told me back then that in 2012 the worst thing I was going to be doing was driving without a license, I would have laughed so hard I would have fallen off the jail bench.

Even after I cleaned up and Miguel (and my mother and my father and pretty much everyone else) pestered me to get a valid driver's license, the cost seemed prohibitive. I had a huge thirty-three hundred dollar fine from Hawaii, plus a four hundred dollar defensive driving class I was supposed to take from an accident in Florida, in addition to a few fines here and there from California. It was a lot and I'd have to deal with each state individually.

The result was that I occasionally thought about getting my license, but then never did anything about it. Getting my license felt like a pesky task that would also be a huge financial hit. Paying those fines when Miguel and I had so many other financial obligations seemed stupid. After all, I wasn't going to get anything from it that I didn't already have. I was driving anyway. Once those fines were paid, what were they going to tell me—Oh, now you can drive for reals.

So I continued not to pay them.

But at this point, driving without a license really was the worst thing I was doing, and that started eating away at me. Not only was I driving myself to church every week—in essence breaking the law to get to church—but I was also giving rides to other people. What if I got pulled over and someone learning about the church saw that I was driving illegally? What kind of example would that set?

Finally, Miguel and I decided that we would dig out some money to pay my fines and get my license back. Easy, right?

Wrong.[1] It wasn't easy. And it definitely wasn't quick. But one by one, I paid my fines and got my license cleared in Florida and California. When I finally got Hawaii paid off, they told me, "Oh, just because you paid the fine doesn't mean you'll necessarily get your license back."

Excuse me. What exactly did it mean?

In order to get my license, I had to write the licensing division of Hawaii a physical letter, asking for my license to be re-instated. I felt like a contestant on *The Bachelor*. They could either accept or reject my letter and my groveling. And if they rejected it, well, that was that, and I'd still be without a legal license, minus four thousand bucks.

I wrote my letter anyway. Several weeks later, I received

papers in the mail saying that my license was no longer suspended.

I still had to take my driver's test though. Like any sixteen-year-old. And, just like a sixteen-year-old, I diligently studied the little test booklet and took the little test. I passed. So, I made an appointment to take my driving test and got a grouchy woman from you-know-where. I didn't pass.

I had been driving for thirty years, and during my drug years, I had been intensely careful NEVER to be pulled over. But there I was like a teenage girl, in tears after my driving test. I went home and called my mother.

I had to wait two more weeks to take it again. I was too embarrassed (and annoyed) to go back to the same DMV, so this time I went to a DMV on the other side of town, and passed my test.

They took my picture, gave me a paper copy of my license and then, like any proper DMV, made me wait several more weeks before receiving my actual legit driver's license in the mail.

When it finally came, I was so happy. I called my mother again to tell her the news.

And then I called Phoebe. Because now it was time to get Phoebe's license taken care of. That's right, my daughter didn't have a proper driver's license either. She didn't have a completely defunct license like I did, but she'd been driving with a Louisiana license ever since she'd come to Indiana and she had her own mini chunk of fines to pay off.

We paid the fines and got her license switched to the correct state. For the first time in Phoebe's life, both mother and daughter had valid driver's licenses.

You can call me Squeaky.[2]

ASIDE FROM MY NOW-CLEAN CONSCIENCE, I DIDN'T EXPECT my new license to affect me. After all, I had been driving for most of my life without it. But about a year after getting my license, I was driving and my GPS fell on the floor. I reached down to pick it up and, as I did, the light in front of me turned red. I didn't see it. I cruised through that light, hitting a car that was coming from the other direction. Both cars jammed to a stop, airbags deployed, my head whacked back against the seat.

When the cops opened my door and helped me untangle from the air bag, they'd probably never seen somebody so happy to be in an accident in all their lives. Because when they asked for it, I could whip out my shiny new license for them to run through their computers.

As the dust settled (mostly figuratively), I began to worry about the people in the other car. "Oh my gosh," I said. "I need to check on them. I hope they're alright." I felt horrible. People around me were telling me not to go over to them. The cop looked right at me and said, "Don't say *anything*." But I had to. It had been my fault and I had to apologize to them. I went over to the elderly couple whose car I'd hit and said, "I'm so sorry I hit you. It was totally my fault. I reached down for something. I'm so so sorry."

The cops were probably ready to wrap me up in a straight jacket and carry me away. But the couple looked at me and replied, "It means so much to us that you apologized."

We exchanged numbers and insurance information. The man's arm was hurting, so they took him to the hospital in an ambulance, and Phoebe came to pick me up.

A few days later, I couldn't stop thinking about them. I called them up and said, "I just wanted to make sure you guys are alright."

The man, Paul, had a broken arm, which made me feel

terrible. But his wife, Martha, assured me that they were going to be okay, and that they really appreciated that I had told them I was sorry. "We're just happy to be alive," Martha said. "In a few weeks we'll be celebrating our 50th wedding anniversary."

I was really glad I hadn't killed them.

A few days later, I went to their house and dropped off a home-faked dinner that I'd bought at the store along with some muffins that I'd gotten them for breakfast. "I just wanted to make your life a little easier," I said.

We talked about our churches, and they told me that in a few weeks Paul would be honored at a ceremony at the new high school, which was dedicating a music hall to him.

Somehow I wound up invited to the ceremony[3].

At the dedication of the music hall, I met their family. We were friends now. Good thing too. Their son was the leader of the SWAT team in Evansville. I thought about how differently it would have played out if I'd been an angry addict with no license who had hit them, instead of an apologetic Christian with a barely-used, perfectly legal driver's license in hand. We wouldn't be friends. I wouldn't have been celebrating with them and their SWAT team son at the dedication of the music wing at the local high school.

Because I would have been locked in a cell, awaiting bail so I could start all over again. And then again. And again.

Instead, after the ceremony, I walked out to my perfectly legal car with my perfectly legal license, and drove home. That's not something that makes most people marvel. But I did. I was a woman who didn't have to check her taillights or make sure her blinker was working. I was a woman who didn't have to hide anything that was in her purse. I was a woman who didn't even have to stop at the gas station for a pack of cigarettes or a cup of coffee.

Almost every piece of me from my ankle to my clothes to the way I smelled was different now.

I was a woman I was just getting to know. And I loved her.

———————

AFTER SEVERAL YEARS ATTENDING CHURCH, AFTER GETTING baptized, after quitting bad habits and trying to develop good ones, after years of finding excuses and feeling inadequate, I decided it was time to talk to my bishop about going to the temple. Anyone can walk off the streets into a church building for the Church of Jesus Christ of Latter-day Saints, but temples are different. The temple is considered a sacred space, a retreat from the world, a place of contemplation and commitment making. To keep it a sacred place, members of our church prepare seriously before entering what we consider a very holy place[4]. Going to the temple felt scary. I was worried I would "fail" at it, like I had failed at so many other things. But it turns out, it's not something you succeed or fail at. It's a place where a person can make promises to God, promises that you try hard to keep. This doesn't mean you're perfect, only that you're trying. I was definitely trying.

Within the church, I had a visiting teaching route and a calling. Which are just Mormon-y ways of saying I did different types of work and service in the church. I tried to help other addicts who were learning about the church and meeting with the missionaries. I gave people rides and took meals or gifts when I could.

———————

1. Um, have you met the DMV? This process was like your last DMV visit on steroids.

2. Because I was so squeaky clean in case you didn't get it.
3. Like a proper Mormon stalker.
4. It's difficult to find a perfect comparison for these temples. There are some similarities to ancient Jewish temples, although there are many differences as well. And although completely different than a Native American vision quest, preparing to attend a temple is similar in that you are trying to prepare yourself for a deeper spiritual experience both in the moment and in the future. It could be considered a spiritual rite of passage. Attending the temple and making promises to God there is intended to move you forward in your spiritual life.

CHAPTER TWENTY-THREE

I was still not a perfect woman. And, unfortunately, it was becoming clear that I was still not in a perfect marriage.

Miguel's health had begun to decline. His kidneys, which had been an issue for years needed to be replaced. We'd been to the doctor to see if I would be a suitable donor. I was. It seemed life would continue on in relative security for us.

Miguel was still working overseas for months at a time. Lately when we talked, he had again begun to retreat into himself, acting aloof, sometimes even mean. I could feel in my heart that something was going on. When he came home, he was very sick and I overheard him talking to a woman on video chat. I'd been here before[1]—different woman, different situation, same story. And I was furious. I had been planning to give him my kidney, and this was how he thanked me.

But this time, I did not lie down and drink myself into a stupor. I didn't visit my friend and cry myself to pieces and spend the next two days in bed. I consulted with an attorney. I still didn't want a divorce. But I did want a husband I could trust, and I knew that I couldn't control what Miguel did. Nor did I want to. If we had to get divorced, we would get divorced. I no longer worried about money or possessions. I no longer worried about whether people would love me. I knew I had a daughter and friends who loved me deeply. I knew that I could get a job serving people who were elderly or sick. I did that for free much of the time anyway. And I knew that I didn't need to live large. Miguel had sometimes held money over my head, had sometimes reinforced the idea that I had nowhere to go if not with him. But now, with my church friends and support group, with a confidence that a loving God was aware of me, I knew I did. I could make it.

Miguel returned to the states to receive the medical help he needed.

And proceeded to almost die.

The old Laura—she wouldn't have cared. She might even have laughed. *Serves you right, sucker. That's what you get for cheating on this girl.*

But the new Laura was a different woman, one I barely recognized.[2] I mean, don't get me wrong, a part of me wanted to walk out the door and leave Miguel to deal with everything on his own. Before Mormon Laura would have done that in a second, with some choice words to boot. But the new Laura couldn't bring herself to do it.

Miguel's kidneys were failing. And, it turns out, his heart was too. He went in to the hospital to have a stent put into his artery so he could proceed with a kidney transplant, but when they put the dye in, they realized that he would need triple bypass surgery.

Even a normal recovery would have taken months, but Miguel didn't have a normal recovery. When he came home, he couldn't breathe right. After that, he got vertigo and had to be hospitalized again. Home. Hospital. Home. Hospital. Home. Hospital. For three months[3].

He couldn't walk and began throwing up violently. Back

to the hospital. They pumped him up with fluids. Home again. His left lung filled with fluid and he got an infection in his chest. Back to the hospital. The doctor prescribed a lot of steroids. He returned home. They told him the medicine would cause side effects so we didn't worry right away when he got sicker. And sicker. And then so sick that we went back to the hospital to find out that he had C. diff[4], which is life threatening in eleven percent of the cases. Miguel was definitely one of that eleven percent. In fact, each and every thing from the bypass surgery to the pneumonia to the C. diff was life threatening; and he couldn't seem to recover from one before another struck.

At one point, he was so weak, he couldn't even lift the blanket off the bed. If he was hot or cold, I or a nurse would need to move the blanket to try to make him comfortable. He had mouth moisturizers, but he was so exhausted and frail, he couldn't squeeze them into his mouth himself. Instead, he would open his mouth like a tiny baby bird and I would give them to him. He lost fifty pounds in three months.

We both thought he would die. The doctors did, too. My brother came into town to help him prepare his last will and testament, and to say goodbye. Miguel was so weak that Randy had to lift him up in his bed in order to do this. Miguel couldn't walk; he couldn't eat. "I'm ready," he said. "I want to see my son and my grandfather." But I guess he wasn't ready enough.

Neither was I. At first, as his health declined, I did only what a decent human being would have done (which was still way better than what Before Mormon Laura would have done). I took him to his appointments. I made sure he was safe and well and clean. As things got worse and his need became greater, I stayed by his side more and more, almost constantly, my heart softening as I watched him suffer, as I tried to ease his suffering the best I could. He pleaded with me not to leave his side, and I didn't. Make no mistake—I know that I didn't *save* Miguel. But I did care about him. I did care for him.

And then, bit by bit, step by step, he began to improve.

If I had left, or even if I'd stayed, but had ignored his needs both physically and emotionally, I believe that Miguel might have given up, that he might have died. If he had, I would have gotten everything financially. But that's not what I wanted. I wanted to be there for someone who needed me. When you have loved someone for so long, it is hard to give up on him. Especially when you have learned to love in a better, stronger way.

Love alone, however, is not always enough to keep two people together. Especially when it starts to feel one-sided. Miguel thanked me for all my help. Honestly, earnestly. I forgot for a while about getting divorced. I thought we would make it. Maybe he did too. I don't know. But as he started to feel better, he drifted back to his old habits (the ones he had when there was someone else in his life). He was not always nice to me. It might even be fair to say he was not often nice to me. There was still another woman across the ocean and I believe the temptation of a beautiful, potentially wealthy other woman called to him. I'm sure it was easy for him to believe that she would be better than me in so many ways.

In the end, it was a small thing that broke me—something that might not have mattered under different circumstances. After I fell asleep one night, Miguel went through my phone.

I woke up to go to the bathroom and he began criticizing me for the few texts I'd sent when I had been planning to divorce him[5]. I hadn't felt the anger and hurt expressed in those texts in the last three months. But listening to him rail on me, I realized it was over.

I couldn't drag him along with me. If he couldn't forgive and love me for some hurt words when I was willing to love and forgive him for being the cause of those words, if he couldn't look past a few texts when I was willing to look past multiple affairs, if he couldn't bring himself to talk nicely when I had stayed by his bedside for the last three months, when I had fed him, clothed him, bathed him, helped him to the bathroom, if he couldn't reach out to me after all of that, then there wasn't a lot I could do to change him. Or us.

The realization came with some sadness (and, yes, plenty of anger), but not with the desperation I'd felt earlier in our marriage. Instead of panic and inadequacy, I felt an incredible sense of peace, happiness even. I knew that God, my friends, and the church would watch over me[6]. I knew I could move forward and—I hoped—upward.

---

1. Twice actually. In addition to the positive paternity test woman, Miguel had at least one other affair while overseas.
2. I'm not saying I didn't have my moments. I was very angry and very hurt. I may have bought myself some divorce-party gifts before Miguel came home and started to die. I may have called and texted some friends, relieved that the failing relationship was finally ending. But I was still so different from the old me as to be almost unrecognizable.
3. Within those three months, he was only able to be home for eleven days.
4. C. difficile infection. A bacterium that can cause diarrhea and inflammation to the colon.
5. The texts were from three or four months earlier—he'd had to go back that far to find something negative. I'm not saying that sending angry, hurt texts about your unfaithful spouse is a GOOD idea, only that it is

natural and human. It's something I did. It's something I thought was over.

6. I knew that even if I couldn't be loved, honored, and cherished by my husband, I could be loved, honored, and cherished by the missionaries and by my friends in the church.

CHAPTER TWENTY-FOUR

S everal years after I joined the church, my mother died. While I had been addicted to drugs, we had walked a rough road. Who am I kidding? We had dragged along with our butts in the gravel.

She had spent years praying and worrying and losing sleep over me. She had been the one to take me to the doctor's office the time I'd learned I was pregnant. She had been the one to send the ambulance when I had called her before trying to commit suicide. She had been the one to play the tough love card and tell me (and the judge) that she wouldn't take Phoebe. She had been the one to suffer my most intense and personal silences. She had been the one I had struggled with more than anyone to see eye to eye.

My mother had been a long-time Christian and I can now only imagine the prayers and tears and sleeplessness I must have caused her. She had been thrilled to see me join a Christian church, even if it wasn't the same as her Christian church. By the time she died, we had enjoyed several years of sweet healing as mother and daughter. I would visit her and my step-father regularly. I was even able to help her when my step-father got heart surgery. It felt so good to be the one helping instead of being helped. I also met the ladies in her prayer circle—the women who had prayed for me *for years* when I'd been on drugs. We'd go out to lunch together. Every time the vacation ended and I went back to Indiana, Mom and I would both be in tears, not wanting to leave one another. Things had been really good.

Even so, I flew home after her funeral feeling deflated. I had been doing so well, but now I found that it was hard for me to shake the feeling that there was still that little part of my life that couldn't quite be fixed. A mean little voice inside of me kept saying that I had disappointed her hopelessly, forever-ly. Those few getting-better years hardly seemed enough to balance out all the hard-and-sharp-as-icicle ones. Our problems and pasts had just been too disappointing and life had been too short.

Several months later, I bought a CD of Carrie Under-wood's Greatest Hits. I was a fan and particularly enjoyed some of her more Christian-themed songs like "Jesus Take the Wheel" and "Something in the Water." He had taken my wheel and there had definitely been something in the water for me. But as I got to the end of her second CD, I heard a song that I hadn't expected, a song I had never heard her sing.

From the speakers in my car came the clear, achingly strong words to "How Great Thou Art."

It was my mother's favorite song.

I felt in that moment that my mother was there underneath the words, that she was telling me, "It's okay, Laura. You're doing just fine."

She was right.

Then sings my soul, my Savior God to thee,
How great thou art, how great thou art.
Then sings my soul, my Savior God to thee,
How great thou art, how great thou art.

To appoint unto them that mourn in Zion, to give unto them
beauty for ashes, the oil of joy for mourning, the garment of
praise for the spirit of heaviness.

— ISAIAH

61:3

Beauty for ashes. New life. From dust.

EPILOGUE

Two years before I joined the church, I had written a letter to Dr. Phil, begging him to help me with my relationship with my daughter. I told him that I'd gone through so much to get my daughter back, but that now I just felt like she hated me. I told him all about my drugs, about losing Phoebe, about getting her back, about the fights. I told him that I knew I'd screwed up royally, that I knew I'd made a thousand mistakes, but I just wanted to know how I could repair our relationship. I didn't hear back and, soon enough, I forgot that I'd written at all.

Then, about two years after I'd joined the church, I started getting calls on my cell phone from Burbank Studios. I assumed it was a wrong number. But they called and called and called. Finally, one day when I was out shopping, I absent-mindedly answered the phone.

"Hi. This is Macie from the Dr. Phil show."

Um, hello.

Turns out they were doing a spinoff show called *The Test*. "We'd love to fly you and your daughter out to California to be on it," Macie was saying in her sweet, cheerful voice.

I stopped in the store, took a quick look at my decent little life, and laughed. "Sorry, honey," I told her. "You're too late. I don't need it anymore."

For a minute, there was a pause on the other end of the line. "You know what," she told me. "You're the first person I've called who's turned me down. Everyone else is still having problems."

"Not me," I said. "I'm Mormon now." Which didn't mean I didn't have problems, of course. Which didn't mean Phoebe and I didn't have problems. I just didn't make them so much bigger than they needed to be anymore.

And since I was being so helpful, I told her, "Tell those people, next time they see those missionaries riding by on their bikes, they need to flag them down."

"I can't do that," she said. "I'd be out of a job."

We both laughed. And talked for about forty minutes while I wandered around the store, not getting any shopping done. At the end of our conversation, she said, "I'm really happy for you. I'm glad things are going better."

I was too.

And, yes, that show did eventually air. And, yes, I did watch it. And, yes, I was extremely glad not to be on it.

AFTERWORD

BY JEAN KNIGHT PACE

I met Laura when we were both leaders in the women's group at our church. She looked like a normal, middle-class house-wife. Which is what she was. But as we got to know each other, it became clear that it wasn't what she'd always been. As I learned about Laura's life, I offered to help her write a book. She wasn't sure she was ready for that, but a year or two later, she approached me. She felt like her story would be able to help people and give them hope. She especially thought it would be good for addicts or their families—those people who aren't sure their son, daughter, sister, brother, or friend will ever come back. Laura wanted to tell them that they could.

And so we began digging into Laura's past. Some of it wasn't pretty. While I was in the middle of some of the heav-iest writing of this book—Laura was constantly getting arrested, her daughter in foster care, her leg so bad she could barely walk, her life often threatened (at both gun point and knife point) by people who should have been her friends—Laura called me asking if I'd do her a favor.

She had prepared "Twelve Days of Christmas" baskets for

someone new to our church. She wondered if my kids and I would be willing to secretly drop off a few of them for her. "I need someone who can ding dong ditch, not leave and limp," she told me.

Laura asked if we would do just a few of the days. She gave us gorgeously arranged baskets, filled with generous amounts of baubles and goodies, as well as one piece of a nativity set each night.

When she dropped the packages off at our house, she'd often have goodies for my kids too (and not a few). Then, on our assigned nights, my kids and I drove through the dark on a covert mission.

Dropping off secret gifts at Christmastime, I found it hard, almost impossible, to believe that this beautiful woman giving us baskets overflowing with the temporal tokens of her love and generosity was the same one who had spent years hopping apartments, evading cops, hanging out in holding cells, sleeping in jail beds, being beaten half to death, snorting lines of powder into her nose through straws and bits of rolled paper just so she could get through the day.

And then one night, when the coast wasn't clear for us to do our drop off, we drove around the neighborhood, looking at Christmas lights until we finally stopped at a large Catholic church. It was tall with stain glass windows, lit up for the season. My kids and I looked at pictures of Christ and his apostles, his death and resurrection. It was then that I realized Laura wasn't the same woman at all. Not only had her habits changed, but her heart had as well—her thoughts, her desires, her impulses. Laura hadn't been washed off or repaired by Christ. She had been rebuilt, renewed, reformed. New life from ashes, fleshy heart from stone (1 Cor. 11:19).

It hadn't happened in a moment or an event. It had happened in the ups and downs of days, through weeks and years, across decades. It can happen to all of us as we stagger towards change, as we stumble to put one foot in front of the other, as we reach out and take His hand.

Half an hour later, when we were finally able to drop off Laura's Christmas basket, I realized that in hearing Laura's story, in letting it sink in, in seeing the new woman born from an old creature, I had been changed too (Mosiah 27: 25-26).

ACKNOWLEDGMENTS

Several people kept me from being on a spinoff of The Dr. Phil show. It's time to thank them.

First, I need to thank my mom and dad for never walking away (even though that's what any sane person would have done). I also appreciate my wonderful step-father and step-mother for the support they've given over the years.

Thank you, Sabra, for keeping my daughter safe when I couldn't.

Jan Ketchel, thank you for doing a thankless job (I know that back in my drug years I never had any intention of thanking you for anything), and for standing up for me in court after I pulled myself together.

A huge life-changing thank you to Dr. Peter Newton and the rest of the staff at UC San Diego for being willing to do an experimental procedure on my leg. It still works! You are saints, all of you.

I need to thank my long-time neighbor and best friend, Donna Jones, who saw me through marriage problems, family problems, and life problems. And who then saw me change and celebrated the good times with me as well.

Thank you to my nephew, Danny and his wife, Diana, for not being intimidated by your crusty aunt and sending the missionaries my way. Also, thanks for showing me an example of what a life and family could look like. Thank you to my niece, Lindsay, my nephews, Shaun and Michael, and to my great nieces and nephews. You all inspire me!

Sister Potter and Sister Kaulkman. Thank you for showing up at our door and speaking Spanish to Miguel. Thank you for being my "Mormon therapists" and leading me to a better way of life. I'd also like to thank all the other missionaries who have influenced me over the years, helped me move things, served me in dozens of ways. There are too many of you to name here, but thank you.

Sally Daetwyler, you were my first church (and churchy) friend. Thank you for welcoming me in. Thank you for never judging me. Thank you for the day when I said, "I'm not like you guys. I once beat up a grown man." And you just responded, "But you're not that person anymore."

Thank you to my mentors and wonderful role models who have taught me how to find happiness through Christ. Thank you to Ed Daetwyler (Sally's husband). Thank you to Toni and Tom VanWormer who have been there for me through everything. I could not be this happy without you two in my life. Thank you to Dan and Christi Patrick and Ruth and Byron Halling who had such a strong influence on me with their love and guidance. Thank you to the amazing Cushing family. There are many, many more church friends who have influenced and inspired me over the years. Thank you to the entire Evansville Ward. I can't include everyone in this list, but thank you so much.

Jean—thank you for helping me get my story onto the page, for capturing my feelings from those times, and for not running off when you heard some of the things I had to tell.

Thank you, Randy, from the bottom of my heart. Thank you for never giving up on me. Thank you for your constant love, support, and guidance over the years. You still continue to help me to this day.

And a final—and most important—thank you to my beautiful, amazing daughter who has gone through this crazy life with me. From the minute you arrived, you were my light in the darkness, the reason I had to keep trying.

Laura Andrade has had many jobs, only a few of them legal. She is a former bartender, babysitter, and drug dealer. She now works as an elder caregiver. When she is not telling people her story, she enjoys talking with friends and taking people to lunch.

Jean Knight Pace is the co-author of the fantasy novels, *Grey Stone* and *Grey Lore* and the author of the memoir, *Hugging Death: Essays on Motherhood and Saying Goodbye*.